Head For The Cloud

Anecdotes, Adventures and Scotland's Munros

Head For The Cloud

Anecdotes, Adventures and Scotland's Munros

Sue Pugh

Illustrations by Steve Conway
sc-artworks.co.uk

© Sue Pugh, 2016

Published by Pugh Stones

A CIP catalogue record for this book is available from the British Library.

ISBN 978-0-9954899-0-5

Illustrations © Steve Conway

Book layout and cover design by Clare Brayshaw

Front cover: Inaccessible Pinnacle
Back cover: Fionn Bheinn

Prepared and printed by:

York Publishing Services Ltd
64 Hallfield Road
Layerthorpe
York YO31 7ZQ

Tel: 01904 431213

Website: www.yps-publishing.co.uk

CONTENTS

Acknowledgements

There have been many people who have helped me along the way, particularly when I had serious doubts about telling my story.

Good friends and work colleagues have encouraged me, but also offered constructive criticism which has helped me pursue my quest. Even a stranger with considerable professional knowledge, and who I've never met, has channelled his opinions to help me achieve my goal!

Thank you to Anita and Carl who've been so supportive and kindly insisted that I told the story "warts and all". We've many memories; we worked as a team and always came out smiling.

I want to express a special thank you to Martin Moran, a well-respected mountaineer and mountain guide. I was just a client of his and yet because of him, my life changed and I have experienced moments I could have only dreamed about. That is something I will never forget.

I'm leaving the most important person to the end and that of course is my dear husband, Dave. None of this would have been possible without him and living a dream with the person you love is what real happiness is all about.

CHAPTER 1

A ROCKY START

'I hate this godforsaken place,' echoed across the hills as my dear husband Dave strode on ahead seemingly totally oblivious to the terrain. We'd crossed a burn without the aid of the basic essential known as a "bridge", and now heather camouflaged potentially ankle-wrenching holes in hidden rocks underfoot.

'Where's the path … WAIT for me,' was my next rant as Dave was getting further and further away. Had I been seven years old rather than forty-seven, my legs would have been slapped for such an outburst. This was not my first experience of Scotland, but if memory served me right, I was damn sure we had walked on paths and had the likes of bridges on previous visits. I resigned myself to having no alternative other than to continue and perhaps the day would improve. Sadly, after reaching the start of the main ascent onto the mountain Beinn Damh, my hopes were dashed once more. We reached what was apparently a buttress and Dave told me we had to 'climb it directly'. I asked the same old question, 'Where's the path and what do you mean, "climb"?' There were no more tantrums but genuine tears as I was yanked by my rucksack to where I felt safe. The mountain had most certainly put me in my place.

Eventually, we returned to the car and on reflection I found myself thinking it hadn't been such a bad experience. At least Beinn Damh wouldn't be forgotten and perhaps I would give Scotland another go.

I was a latecomer to hill-walking, or any kind of physical outdoor pursuits for that matter. I was thirty when persuaded by my first husband to visit the Lake District and walk round Crummock Water and then achieve the dizzy heights of Catbells summit, a popular easy mountain in the Lakes. But life turns on a sixpence (I suppose a five-pence piece these days) and sadly four years later he died suddenly as the result of a heart attack. We had spent a few days in the Lake District, but there was some small comfort in the fact that we had left the Lakes and returned home rather than climbing the mighty Skiddaw. Although there was a considerable age gap between us, this was an untimely death.

After I spent seven years alone apart from living with my two faithful pooches who understood me far better than most humans, I met Dave. I had arrived to join a guided walk at the local railway station. The outdoor life appealed, but items such as a map and compass were pretty alien to me. Big brothers come in handy, and what I regarded as his bizarre interest in trains paid dividends when he handed me a guided walks programme organised by the Friends of the Settle-Carlisle Line.

Dave was a walks leader and I remember seeing him on the platform. It was nearly love at first sight until he opened his mouth. In a broad Yorkshire accent he shouted across to another walker, 'Ay Pete, (the t in Pete was a silent t) ow ya doin'?' None of my imaginary "requirement" boxes for meeting the love of my life received a tick. Dave was the owner of an old Nissan Cherry which looked like paint stripper had been poured over it. I'd always been swayed by the sight of a nice car, better still if the owner wore a uniform. Dave also owned a motorbike, something I definitely didn't approve of and the biking leathers could hardly be regarded as a uniform. However, love works in mysterious ways and 10 months later in November 1997, we married. I became a fan of two wheels and began to enjoy riding pillion on a Super-sports motorbike; 0 to 60mph in 3.5 seconds was an incredible buzz. But a woman has to draw the line at some things in life and travelling in the Nissan Cherry was one; Dave was persuaded to dispose of the said vehicle. He continued to lead walks, particularly in the Lake District. The routes he devised had a reputation for being adventurous and different and you either loved or hated a "Pugh excursion". The hardened few were keen enough to venture further afield with us.

My love-hate relationship with the Scottish mountains had improved slightly in the seven years since the Beinn Damh trauma, but I was appallingly ignorant of the Black Cuillin Mountains on the Isle of Skye. This was possibly a blessing as had I known the area was a favourite playground of rock climbers and mountaineers alike, I doubt I would have ever set foot there. But my lemming instinct of following my dear husband in the mountains tended to overrule all rational thoughts.

My first sight of the infamous Inaccessible Pinnacle, which forms part of the Cuillin range, was in October 2009 when our friends had joined us for a few days on Skye. It was to be my first major walk after recovering from surgery on my leg. Four months earlier I had fallen off an insignificant stile in the Lake District, en route to a hill called Great Cockup (quite apt), which resulted in Keswick Mountain Rescue coming to my aid. Full marks to them for their professionalism, but so embarrassing to have required their help on terrain your granny could have managed. That nondescript stile, grassy field and easy on the eye scenery would be a far cry from the environment I was about to sample on the Cuillin.

A typical October misty morning greeted us as we set off from Glen Brittle. All too soon the soft easy ground we had enjoyed at the start of the walk was superseded by stones, scree and rock with little vegetation to be seen. The unrelenting ground was fast becoming tedious and I was beginning to wonder whether I could get excited about a lump of rock stuck on top of a mountain. Would it even be visible through the mist which had now enveloped us? Dave had prattled on about the Inaccessible Pinnacle and how I would be impressed at the sight of it. He'd climbed it a few years earlier, persuading his friend Allan it would be fun.

After pointing at various large formations here and there, enquiring, 'Is that it?' (not unlike a child whinging to its parents, 'Are we there yet?') and the only reply from Dave being a chuckle, I kept walking. Some two hours later, having traipsed up a mountain side, where I could see sod all and with my "war wound" from the stile incident beginning to twinge, the Inaccessible Pinnacle appeared out of the mist. I stopped dead in my tracks and looked in total disbelief at this less than appealing sight; it was a monster of a rock. With all sincerity I announced to Dave and our friends, 'You won't get me up that'. I was remembering that a particular past encounter on rock had hardly been a match made in heaven. Let me explain.

There's a mountain by the name of Ben Arthur, also known as The Cobbler. We visited it in 2008 when my confidence had grown just a little too quickly. It was a breezy day with the odd squally sleet shower blowing in and out. The home of the main summit has a rocky outcrop which stakes its claim as the true summit. It's accessed by crawling through a hole in the rock (threading the needle) that leads to a narrow ledge with a drop of perhaps 100ft, then a short scramble is required to reach the summit.

Dave went to climb to the true summit while I waited for him with some friends. For some unknown reason I got a bee in my bonnet that I was going to give it a go. Dave was oblivious of my intentions, in fact he'd been to the top and was on his way down when I appeared on the ledge. He managed to utter the words, 'Wait, I'll come and give you a hand,' but sadly my new-found confidence had gone to my head. 'I'm fine, I'll give it a go,' was my reply and I started to climb. The next thing I knew I was falling backwards. My rucksack cushioned the impact on my back and my legs were dangling in thin air over the ledge but luckily the rest of me was in relative safety. A most ridiculous conversation then followed:

Dave: 'What did you do that for?'
Sue: 'For the Hell of it … of course!'
Dave: 'You've broken the golden rule – three points of contact.'
Sue: 'Yes, I know I've broken the ******** rule, but I didn't mean to!'
Dave: 'Are you OK?'
Sue: 'Yes.'

When I saw where I could have ended up, it did provide food for thought and it wasn't until the following day before I realised how my foolish actions had impacted on me. My confidence was well and truly shattered. Perhaps I should thank the mountain for the wake-up call as The Cobbler was nearly the last.

The Inaccessible Pinnacle, also known as the In Pinn or Pinn, holds the title of being the only Munro which requires rock climbing skills to reach the summit. For those of you (like me, not that long ago) who don't know what a Munro is, I'll try to explain. A Munro is a Scottish mountain over 3,000ft high. Just to confuse the issue, there are other tops over 3,000ft but they're regarded as subsidiary peaks and therefore do not hold the Munro classification.

We chose to eat our sandwiches in close proximity to the Pinn. Whether we were admiring it I'm not too sure, but I had lost my appetite which seemed ridiculous as we'd only gone to take a look. The sight of this object made me feel decidedly uncomfortable but I couldn't take my eyes off it. I was staring at "it" and "it" was staring back. What lay before me was totally beyond my comprehension. This wasn't a mountain; it was a pillar of rock suitably named "Inaccessible". Thank heavens I was clueless when Dave and Allan had climbed the Pinn and incredible that Allan still regarded Dave as a friend. The Pinn won the staring game. I gave in, the cheese and grape sarnies remained untouched, and with my tail between my legs, I slunk away.

I never gave the Pinn any further thought until several months later when Dave and I were watching a TV programme, "Munro Mountain Man". It explained the history of the Munros but also featured Nicholas Crane climbing the Pinn with mountain guide Martin Moran. I was perched on the edge of my seat with butterflies in my stomach, but at the same time making a note of Martin's name. Why was I doing this? I had no conscious intention of re-acquainting myself with another staring match because I knew who would win. But deep down an embryonic niggle had set seed. The programme had certainly struck a chord. Alan Hinkes, a top class mountaineer, who also featured on the same programme, made a comment, 'a determined approach is required'. Little did I know how often I would be reminded of that philosophy in the years ahead.

Dave and I continued to visit Scotland, returning to some favourite mountains and venturing to pastures new. Two years later the Inaccessible Pinnacle seed had matured and in May 2012 I had an inexplicable need to climb it. Dave had said he would take me, but I felt that this serious expedition warranted the luxury of a professional guide for safety reasons, and also to ensure that a mountain was not cited in divorce proceedings. I asked Anita, one of our walking friends, if she would care to join me. I thought she may be interested and we were of a similar ability. I didn't want extra pressure from the company of someone who was more proficient than me – excluding mountain guides of course.

I found a crumpled piece of paper in my purse with Mr Moran's name on and emailed him. Looking back at that message, I do wonder if many clients ramble on with such superfluous detail. As is my tendency in life, I err on the side of unnecessary information. God forbid if I ever have to be subjected to questioning by a clever barrister; they would make mincemeat of me. Did I really need to state that I was short with dark hair and Anita tall with blonde hair, that we lived in Yorkshire, that I worked part-time, oh, and by the way, I had concerns about reaching for footholds and handholds and Anita didn't like exposure? I managed to stop short of stating what train I commuted on and what my favourite colour was.

It was September before we actually sorted out a date and due to a spell of unsettled weather the arrangements were last minute. In fact, they were finalised while attending my father-in-law's funeral. Mixed emotions were the order of the day, remembering old Gilbert, listening to the vicar, and mentally checking the handles were level on the coffin (I'd previously worked in the funeral business for 20 years). At the same time, I felt my stomach churn thinking of that rock celebrity perched on the Cuillin Ridge waiting to see what I was made of. I remember when speaking to Martin that day (from the funeral tea) he asked if we would also like to climb Sgurr Mhic Choinnich, a neighbouring Munro. The thought had never entered my head, surely the Pinn was enough for anyone in one day? Such innocence. Unfortunately, due to work commitments, Dave couldn't accompany me to Skye and be privy to the new rock climber extraordinaire in action, but perhaps this was for the best.

Anita and I arrived on Skye in good spirits, a little nervous but rather excited at the prospect of an adventure. We dropped our bags at our B&B and headed to the Sligachan Hotel, just a five-minute drive away. A variety of old photographs of mountains and mountaineers furnished the bar area. On previous visits I had never taken much notice, but this time they all seemed of new significance.

The alarm was set for the following morning, which was totally unnecessary as of course we were wide awake … I wonder why. The lady at the B&B cheerily took our breakfast order, commenting on what a lovely sunny morning it was. I have no idea why either of us ordered a cooked breakfast as very little was eaten. We apologised for the amount we had left even though I did my best to cut the food up and randomly move it about the plate thinking it might appear less. Our hostess didn't mind and said her Labrador would be more than happy we'd lost our appetites. She knew what we were planning and that we'd be heading to Glen Brittle to start the adventure. It turned out she had lived in the area for many years and still remembered seeing the rescue teams bringing bodies off the mountains. But she assured us we would be fine.

On the drive to Skye we had played a CD by M People and one track seemed quite appropriate, "Search for the Hero". So after breakfast, while waiting to be picked up by our mountain guide, I found myself listening to the music, searching for that "determined approach", interrupted by several visits to the bathroom. The thought of the In Pinn to a non-climber rivals any laxative on the market.

Martin arrived, we exchanged pleasantries and off we went with the mountains looking splendid in the glorious weather. At last we were on the road. Do you agree that it's the waiting prior to events that's always the worst?

We parked opposite a mountain rescue hut, no doubt a pure coincidence. Or was it an omen? It was at this stage we were asked if we'd brought a map. I had a pair of waterproof trousers, a fleece, a spare pair of knickers, all items which may well have been put to good use, but a map? Anita and I looked at one another and replied in the negative. Surely a mountain guide should know the way and would have his own map? Oh dear, this did not bode well. (No need to start writing to the authorities. Of course he knew exactly what he was doing and was fully equipped!)

A nice steady pace was set as we left the safety of the car. Anita in particular was relieved we had good weather as that had been one of her stipulations for climbing the Pinn. We knew there was about a two-hour walk before we would reach the Pinnacle, but this was a two-edged sword. It gave us time to ease ourselves into the day and enjoy our surroundings, yet there was the urge to get to the nitty-gritty sooner rather than later. Perhaps I was nervous because I had seen the Pinn back in 2009. However, Anita hadn't been there that day. Of course nobody was forcing me to be here and at any time I could say no, but there was something inside my head which wouldn't allow this.

Anita and I chatted away to Martin, taking it in turn speaking about this and that. I didn't envy Martin's job as a mountain guide when it came to making polite conversation with Joe Public. He must have some clients he would prefer to push off a mountain. I know my days of patience, tolerance and understanding seem to have virtually evaporated with the passing of time.

We'd been walking for about an hour before we stopped and were instructed to wear our helmets in readiness for the rougher ground up ahead. This was a new carry on to me, wearing a helmet for a walk, or even scrambling for that matter. However, the merits of helmets being worn were explained. As I was fumbling, trying to fasten the chin strap on my helmet with my less than steady hands, I happened to look around and noticed a change in the weather. There were clear skies over Glen Brittle with the blue sea shimmering in the sunshine, but a dark grey blanket was fast approaching from the opposite direction. By the time we reached the Pinn I could not only hear rain, but also feel sleet pitter-pattering on top of my helmet. Inwardly, I began to panic. If the plug was pulled on the venture I really couldn't face the thought of going through the nerve-wracking palaver of returning at a later date. There was no need to worry as Martin produced a rope from his rucksack and clearly we were to press on. The staring game of 2009 with the Pinn was not on the agenda. I had already decided that the least eye contact possible was a preferable tactic.

We were allowed to leave our rucksacks on the ground, which seemed a good idea as less weight to carry might aid our agility. While we were being "tied up", I glanced at the towering wet black rock, reaching to the dark grey sky. My mouth was dry and my mind blank, and had anyone asked my name I think I would have struggled to answer. Was I really doing this? One pleasant surprise was that we were to climb together. We'd had the naive impression we would be taken up individually and neither of us wanted to be the one waiting behind. Those who understand these things will realise just how green and ignorant we were.

The various knots were explained although I felt this information was totally wasted on us. I wouldn't have known a clove hitch from a figure of eight (I still have my doubts), and at this stage the brain had gone into meltdown. Martin gave us a few basic tips on climbing and the next thing we knew he'd scampered up the rock, not quite never to be seen again, but certainly out of sight. I'd been placed to climb first with Anita following and with strict instructions to keep the rope tight at all times. It was at this stage that Anita repeated her stipulation that she'd agreed to climb in perfect conditions … as the rain and sleet continued to fall.

Dave had invariably been with me for my "hands on" experiences. Now my guiding light was missing and although safe in the knowledge I was tied to a rope, I had to think for myself and route find. I looked back at Anita and her face seemed to mirror my thoughts. I cast my mind back to what Dave had taught me – I was about to discover whether or not I had paid attention to his words of wisdom. The sooner I could get this over with, the better. The first hitch was making the initial step up to start the climb; this was fast becoming a nightmare. However, once I accepted that there was no escape, and determination would have to be found, slow progress was made.

The size of handholds and footholds is rather subjective. What I regard as a nice sized foothold is totally different to what a climber would think. I was not a climber. I was now putting my faith on a protrusion which may have been about an inch (or in "new money" 2.5cm) wide. This was just big enough to get the toe of my boot on. I must be greedy but there are few things in life where an inch is sufficient, a foothold being one.

By now the rock was cold and wet, which I knew would make everything trickier. I arrived at a particularly awkward section which Dave had warned me about and I'd asked was it easier to the left or the right. I was told there was no left or right, just straight up … he was right.

How I negotiated that section, I haven't the foggiest. I remember wishing my legs were another three or four inches longer, having placed my knee where I never dreamed it would fit. Various text books frown on the use of knees … tough. Whatever part of my anatomy would adhere to the rock was fine by me and would be utilised. At this point I felt there was an uncanny resemblance between me and a limpet, except a limpet might feel pretty confident he will stick to the rock – I was not so sure.

Anita had been watching what line of attack I had taken, but she too was foxed and asked what I had done. I honestly didn't know except that I had placed my knee "somewhere". It's clever how the body can withstand pain without actually feeling it. Try kneeling on a lump of rock and exerting pressure on it; yes, it hurts. Do that on the Pinn and you don't feel a thing.

The vertiginous drops on either side never entered my head. It was not being able to reach good-sized hand or footholds that was alarmingly disconcerting. My fingers were numb with the cold. I hadn't worn normal gloves for fear of losing grip so I had some fingerless gloves on. They were about as much use as a chocolate fireguard. I called to Martin stating it was all becoming too difficult. I was at the end of my tether in more ways than one. Had it been Dave I was calling to, the cloud cover may have still been grey but the air would have definitely been blue! My spirits were lifted as Martin called back that I had just completed the hardest section and with those few words the millstone round my neck loosened its grip.

We had a second section to climb for which I believe the correct term is "pitch". Fortunately, this seemed easier although perhaps more exposed with another alarming drop below, but I could find holds more to my liking. It had seemed like an eternity, but we finally made it and Martin shook our hands. However, there was the small matter of getting back down again with the easiest and quickest option being an abseil down another side of the Pinn.

Anita was to go first so I was instructed to sit down and told not to go anywhere … as if! I was patiently sitting there in my own little world, more or less up in the clouds, when out of the mist a man appeared from behind. He portrayed the archetypal image of a mountaineer, with bushy beard and a little weather-beaten. Remembering my manners I wished him a good morning, but itched to say, 'Do you come here often?' He seemed a charming man, we passed the time of day and he asked if I was with Martin. It was all quite surreal. Here I was on a huge lump of rock, 3,000ft up with only Mother Nature as my neighbour, enjoying a casual conversation, the sort you would normally have waiting in the queue at your local M&S, waiting to return some ridiculous blouse which you knew wouldn't fit in the first place.

In due course it was my turn to abseil down and I'd be exaggerating if I said I enjoyed it; it was acceptable. I'd had a tiny amount of experience with Dave on some small crags in the Yorkshire Dales and had completed a sponsored abseil with the Paras in charge. That was all well and good, but the Pinn was a different kettle of fish. Forcing yourself to lean back and away from the rock face plays havoc with the old brain cells which are screaming and pleading with you to remain upright. But in an unreal world anything is possible. Of course when Martin abseiled off, he whizzed down the rock like Spiderman or some such character with supernatural powers. We re-grouped and enjoyed a celebratory lunch break with a large helping of elation and pride. The bearded man took a photo for us and then Anita and I chatted while Martin spoke to our new friend. He was Andy Nisbet, a legend in mountaineering circles and obviously Martin had great admiration for him.

We were homeward bound, descending into Coire na Banachdich with the car now our destination. The steady pace which was set when we ascended went out of the window. My little legs had never moved so fast, but I didn't mind. I was also taking more direct routes, nearly skipping over obstacles which prior to the adventure I would never have dreamed of doing. My confidence had multiplied tenfold. Anita and I foolishly presumed we would be stopping for a coffee break, but one should never presume. I doubt either of us would have dared to ask for a break, and in any case we would have needed to catch up with Martin in order to ask him! We settled for the elation to quench our thirst.

The sun had the audacity to show its face, but it was immaterial as the day had been a momentous occasion. I loathe people who are constantly texting and checking their phones, but just this once I broke my rule and texted Dave as soon as there was a signal.

I still struggle to choose words which portray how I felt. It seemed I was living in a bubble, the outside world didn't exist and what this bubble had to offer was something quite magical. I was to discover these bubble worlds would become a regular occurrence and disturbingly addictive. Before we bade farewell, Martin asked if we might like to purchase a book he had written, "The Munros in Winter". If I'm honest, I bought a copy as a matter of courtesy. The book was about to change my life.

CHAPTER 2

PLANS ON A POSTAGE STAMP

The bubble of euphoria was still intact as I boarded the 07.37 train to work. I was working in the support/admin sector of a large corporate law firm in Leeds. I hadn't risen to the heady heights of lawyer status, more a "gofer/minion" role. Although I could never be regarded as a bookworm, I couldn't wait for the next train journey to immerse myself in my new book. The Gaelic names meant nothing to me, neither did the detailed information relating to mountains and the technicalities. However, the feeling behind the content was special. Somebody climbing just short of 300 mountains in 83 days, and in winter, sounded an amazing adventure yet totally inconceivable to a lay person. My imagination went into overdrive as I read this extraordinary story, my mind crammed with thoughts and ideas.

The Inaccessible Pinnacle had possibly opened the door to the other Munros. Now I had climbed the most difficult Munro, what was to stop me bagging/climbing all 282 of them? (An unusual expression, "bagging", but that is what it's called.) My attitude to Munro bagging and tick lists was changing from what I once perceived as all the wrong reasons for climbing mountains to a worthwhile venture.

So why all the fuss when the highest Munro, Ben Nevis, is a mere 4,409ft? Not exactly Everest or K2, but unlike footholds, size is not everything. Scotland is exposed to Atlantic and Arctic weather systems resulting in rapidly changing conditions with sub-zero temperatures possible at any time of the year. Waymarked paths, or indeed any kind of path, are few and far between on the vast majority of Scottish mountains. Once away from the popular routes, you can easily walk all day and not see a soul.

I had to consider the logistics and feasibility of what I was thinking; would it be a pipe dream or could I do it? For years I was a follower and although I had progressed considerably from my very early days of walking, I knew for certain it would border on lunacy and sheer irresponsibility to attempt Munro bagging on my own. I needed Dave's full co-operation as he would be responsible for the role of mentor. It would cost a considerable amount of money back and forth to Scotland taking into consideration the mileage and the accommodation, and how many days holiday would be required. I was determined to find solutions.

The first hurdle was cleared as Dave jumped at the idea, even though it would entail repeating numerous Munros that he had already climbed. The financing of the project was courtesy of my late father-in-law. The legacy we had been left could have stayed in a bank account, but where is the fun in that? We were lucky insofar as Dave had taken the opportunity of redundancy which equated to an early retirement. I was working just three days a week so with some effort heading north on a regular basis could work without being totally dependent on holiday leave. It was useful living near Settle in Yorkshire as most areas in Scotland could easily be reached within eight hours or less, and the mileage would be no more than 1,000 miles per trip.

The next decision was a timescale. In order for it to be a challenge I had to be pushing myself mentally and physically and yet I did want to appreciate the mountains. I wasn't starting at zero as I had climbed the princely sum of 49 Munros over a 14-year period; the Pinn was number 49. After some debate we concluded that three years could work well. With 233 still to climb that would average just over 77 a year. This would be a far cry from the likes of Martin Moran and those lovely bearded mountaineers who talk in days and weeks rather than years. However, I was challenging myself and nobody else – easy to say, but would I remember this fact? Another factor in the calculation was that on 31st December 2015 it would be my 60th birthday. What better way to spend the day and the perfect birthday present than on my 282nd Munro.

However, a rather sombre situation had developed in our lives. It was a miserable December evening as we headed to Sunny Scunny. The pouring rain and the glare from oncoming headlights reflecting off the wet tarmac made the car journey even more depressing. We arrived at the care home in Scunthorpe where our dear friend Con had become a resident. Con had been an active man and although 73 years old, could still walk the socks off people half his age. In his younger days he had visited base camp at Everest in an era when such a journey was still a rarity. He was independent, strong willed and at times could be an awkward old cuss. Con had been taken ill with a suspected brain tumour. Within days he had gone from walking and scrambling in the Lake District to becoming bedbound. The prognosis wasn't good and Con was desperate for the end to be sooner rather than later. On previous visits he had asked us to help end his misery; a plea to take him to the Humber Bridge was a favourite.

Con's situation cemented my decision for my challenge. Time is a very precious commodity which all too often is taken for granted. Many of us pay lip service to the "quality and not the quantity" philosophy. We knew time was running out for Con so I told him about the plan to bag all the Munros and that the last one I climbed would be for him. Although Con had lost some ability to speak, he certainly hadn't lost his marbles. He smiled at me and said he would be there … two weeks later Con died.

It was decided to bury Con's ashes in close proximity to Park Fell and Simon Fell in the Yorkshire Dales. It was one of his favourite haunts (excuse the pun), and enjoyed views towards the famous Ribblehead Viaduct on the Settle–Carlisle Railway. This seemed fitting as he had been a fireman on steam locomotives. A large group who had often walked with Con came together for the occasion. People seem wary of cremated remains (ashes) and so I volunteered to carry Con to his final resting place.

At the top of Park Fell we paused awhile for everyone to catch up so I perched myself on my rucksack. Oh dear, I had forgotten about the ashes, and my heart sank as I opened my bag and peered inside. Thank goodness I had only squashed Con a tad and while the container was dented it was intact. I think everyone saw the funny side and it certainly lightened the mood. Dave felt sure Con would have appreciated the experience.

It had been fine talking about our challenge, but we needed to start sooner rather than later and decide on strategy. Theoretically, we could leave any Friday evening and return on a Tuesday. The thought of this freedom was very appealing. We pondered on whether we should concentrate on one area at a time, which would be methodical but perhaps too regimented. I wanted variety and felt that the experience should include some pleasure.

Unfortunately, visiting Scotland and offering regular Lake District walks to our friends would not be feasible. Something had to give, and with a heavy heart the decision was taken to forgo the Lakes. Nonetheless, we promised the annual visits to Scotland would still be on offer. All in all people were understanding, and kindly pointed out that it was our turn to expand our horizons. Many had thanked Dave in the past for taking them to places they would never have imagined possible.

I had envisaged our challenge as something for the two of us. After many happy years of planning so many walks, social events and holidays in a group format, we felt it was time to go it alone for a change. However, the old cogs started whirring and I wondered if Anita might like to join us on some of our trips, after all it was Anita who was there with me for the Pinn. Then a friend by the name of Carl was mentioned who had been with Dave on several winter Scottish trips. How could this work, with Carl in full-time employment and Anita had a husband plus family commitments? We had just lifted our restrictions, but now I could be putting us at the mercy of other people's constraints. All of a sudden things were getting complicated and of my own doing.

After much deliberation we thought it was feasible on the basis that Anita and Carl would need to make their own arrangements whenever they joined us. To be honest, we had no idea if they would like the concept, but without hesitation Anita and Carl jumped at the idea. Most of the potential hitches had been resolved, until Dave pointed out that occasionally we would need to wild camp.

I was 55 years old before I had ever set foot inside a tent and that was only after much persuasion from Dave one sunny day. Roughing it was not in my nature and I couldn't understand how anyone could enjoy themselves without such basic essentials as a flushing loo and their own bedroom, preferably with co-ordinated decor. However, I accepted that I would have to make exceptions if I was to succeed, but it was getting tough before I had even donned a pair of boots.

Although I say we discussed tactics, the detailed plan of action could have been written on the back of a postage stamp. And as for Munro bagging during the winter months, while it was never dismissed it was not discussed. My winter skills would have also fitted on the self-same postage stamp but for the fact that we visited the most unlikely of places, Grange-over-Sands.

Martin Moran was giving a lecture in this small coastal town which was only a good hour's drive from where we lived. Dave had also read the book and was curious, if nothing else, to meet this man. The evening went well, and while I am easily impressed, it takes rather more for Dave to be forthcoming with compliments. Dave was in raptures about what he had seen and heard. Within days the Moran Mountaineering website had been studied and Dave found a winter mountaineering venture suitable for him and Carl. I happened to notice the mention of "overnight in a snowhole" – that sounded interesting. Nevertheless, this was to be a "macho men" break, and at any rate such activities would be way out of my league.

Dave asked me to email Martin. I made it quite clear that the enquiry was purely on behalf of Dave and Carl. Seventy-two hours later and a booking had been made for Dave, Carl … Anita and me. I had been given the green light by Dave and was genuinely surprised that Martin felt it was within my capabilities. All I talked about was the snowhole, with a mental picture of me in a cosy romantic igloo, with tea lights flickering, perched on top of a beautiful mountain. The hard graft and practicalities were totally glossed over. The minor detail, namely the remainder of the itinerary, including climbing snow gullies, never got a look in. An imaginary world had filled the void where brain cells once resided.

CHAPTER 3

SNOW VIRGINS

February 2013

February 2013, the start of my first official bagging year and I find myself in the north-west of Scotland on this winter mountaineering venture.

Day one: practice ice axe self-arrest. I was under the illusion that this would take place on an easy angled incline. There was no obvious sign of a slope that matched this description, only those in the distance that we had walked past. It transpired that we were higher and at a steeper angle due to the condition of the snow; it wasn't particularly slippery. I suppose a bit like the railways with the wrong type of leaves falling. We took Martin's word for it and as instructed, duly threw ourselves down the mountain side. They say an arrest is only 20% successful in a real emergency and it did appear that you travelled some considerable distance before coming to a halt. The motto being, do not slip in the first place.

The next delight was climbing a Grade II snow gully onto the mountain Fuar Tholl situated a few miles from Lochcarron. This was when I wished that I'd paid more attention to the itinerary. I had no idea how I was managing what was asked of me. Perhaps the gully wasn't vertical against a plumb line, but my body felt it was near enough. Whacking an ice axe into the hard snow in order to be upwardly mobile was a thrill. However, having only the front spikes of each crampon shoved into the snow with inconveniently placed bits of rock jutting out was incredibly difficult. I struggled to grasp the theory of how this procedure could work. Surely my foot would come away when the majority of it was in thin air. But then I was never any good at physics. Just for good measure I had to remember not to lift or lower my heel. I was so relieved we had booked on the easiest course. Mercifully, we were roped up and by some miracle I reached the top (or in technical terms I think it is called "topping out"). What an amazing experience – I was grinning like a Cheshire Cat.

* * *

The following day was to be the snowhole experience – the reason I was there in the first place. The mountains had been described as "in condition", whatever that meant, and we were to climb the Forcan Ridge followed by digging a snowhole on The Saddle. The Forcan Ridge is a classic scrambling route leading to The Saddle, a Munro in the Kintail area. With the exception of Carl, the rest of us had previously climbed this mountain and it had been tricky enough without any snow.

The troops were mustered for a kit inspection. Anita and I came out of it quite well, but the same couldn't be said for Carl. The quantity Carl carries is mind boggling. A building manager by trade but very much hands on, he loves his food. Martin was visibly shocked at the volume of Carl's supplies and instructed him in no uncertain terms to whittle it down, while Dave was told to leave a flask behind – it was deemed unnecessary.

It was a pleasant walk before we reached the start of the serious business. Helmets, harnesses and ropes were produced and we were reminded that sloppy crampon work caused accidents. The banter ceased, an uneasy silence descended and the old heartbeat started to race. There were one or two heart-stopping moments when I still found it hard placing my trust in my equipment. However, I had every faith in the rope we were tied to and in Martin, who made it look oh, so easy. The views were picture postcard, blue-pink skies, sun-kissed peaks and the snow fairies had left more than a dusting. I felt very privileged to share such a stage with Nature. We were impressed with the day and how we were managing. However, our guide was less enamoured with our speed or rather lack of speed. The snowhole still required digging and perhaps we hadn't appreciated the time it would take.

The Saddle was reached and the digging commenced. The men took it in turn to dig while Anita and I became the conveyor belt. I'm sure some women could dig as quickly as men, but not in our case. Carl was our guardian angel and his love of pork pies was no drawback. He could dig at an alarming rate, so much so, we couldn't keep up with moving it.

Several hours later and with most of the excavation carried out in the dark, our new home was ready. 15ft long x 8ft wide x 5ft high. I suppose this was the difference between a snowhole and a snowcave. My fairy-tale picture of a snowcave had changed, but not for the worse. It was incredibly hard work but exciting, and Carl was kind enough to discreetly cut different shaped shelves for our tea lights. I was back in one of my

bubble worlds. A well/sink hole had been dug within the cave for the cold air to collect and Dave asked if this could double up as a urinal in the night. The reply was not in the negative but it was pointed out that this would not be the most social of practices.

Because it was 12th February and nearly Valentine's Day I had taken a card for Dave and a packet of M&S chocolate hearts to share. After all, how many people get the chance to open a Valentine's card in a snowcave? I handed the hearts round although I was not too sure if this met with Martin's approval. Was it the fact that:

a) We had strict instructions only to carry essentials? I doubt that chocolate hearts were regarded as essential.

b) Did it appear I wasn't taking it seriously by thinking of such frivolous things?

or

c) Martin was tired after contending with the four of us all day?

I put my money on the latter.

We settled down for the night and my mind drifted back several years to my first attempt at Beinn Alligin in the Torridon Mountains. Snow had been the problem then and the conditions had taken us by surprise. We were ill equipped and we lacked the knowledge or experience, so retreat was the only sensible option. We managed to get as far as Tom na Gruagaich, one of the Munros that forms part of Beinn Alligin. I took one look across to the narrow ridge heading towards Sgurr Mhor, with the Horns of Alligin beyond, and reverse gear was engaged in the blink of an eye. It wasn't the sight of the ridge or the "Horns" that struck the fear of God into me but the white stuff on top of them. The view was stunning but the sickly feeling deep in my stomach told me that was no place for me. We returned at a later date minus the snow and had a wonderful day; Beinn Alligin is now a favourite. Looking at the ceiling of my igloo I would never have imagined how things could change.

I slept surprisingly well despite getting up for a pee in the night which entailed shifting blocks of snow back and forth – our makeshift door. Heavens, it was cold out there. I was still asleep when the alarm went off – yes, an alarm. I wasn't hungry and everything seemed more of an effort, and packing frozen items away was problematic. I had some weird notion that all the hard work was over and it would simply be a case of trotting back down to the car using the easiest route available. I was wrong. We were heading for Sgurr na Sgine, a neighbouring Munro and one that I hadn't done. I was chuffed to be bagging my first Munro of the challenge but concerned that I had little energy. Everything was fine while we were learning more winter skills that didn't require stamina, but things were about to change when we reached an incline. I made, what I thought was, an innocuous comment to Martin, 'I'm tired,' … I got both barrels. 'I've no sympathy. You were offered more casserole last night and refused and you've hardly eaten any breakfast so that's why you've no energy.' Normally, I would be too slow to think of a spur of the moment reply, but I didn't hesitate and snapped back, 'I'm not expecting any sympathy. I'm stating a fact.' Dave seemed taken aback by my response and didn't know what to say, so remained silent, as did Carl and Anita. Every cloud has a silver lining and some good came out of the little contretemps, as I found a new lease of life. I was fuming, silently mouthing obscenities from a distance but gaining speed all the while. My calf muscles were screaming with pain from performing crampon techniques they'd rarely done before, but was I hell as like going to give up.

By the time we reached the summit of Sgurr na Sgine the adrenaline rush had dissipated along with my anger. I was exhausted but pleased at not being defeated. I knew I should have eaten more, but due to my dislike of "performing outside" my tactic was to cut down on bulk which would hopefully eliminate the need to dig a hole. Now how could I have said that, and anyway I would have probably still received a reprimand. However, I had bagged the first Munro of the official challenge in a spectacular way and one I would not forget, me at the age of fifty-seven and Dave knocking on the door of sixty-four – better late than never, I say.

Before heading back down we had a quick break. I was thirsty with nothing left to drink after keeping my supplies to a minimum as instructed. Nobody else seemed to have anything left either. That was until Dave pulled out his flask and handed it round to everyone. As Martin took a swig he looked quizzically at Dave and commented, 'Didn't I tell you to leave this behind?' Dave just smiled as I tried my best to conceal the smug look on my face. I was one very happy but bunged up bunny as the car came into sight, and I wouldn't have missed the experience for the world.

March 2013

It seemed logical to make use of the new winter skills we had learned at the earliest opportunity and while fresh in the memory. The Crianlarich area was chosen with four, possibly five, Munros in mind. An Caisteal , Beinn a'Chroin, Beinn Tulaichean, Cruach Ardrain and Beinn Chabhair.

In order to utilise daylight hours, wild camping was on the menu with the last night in a B&B. The itinerary could hardly be regarded as earth shattering, but with winter conditions and wild camping virginity only recently lost, we needed to be realistic. Anita and Carl were joining us so I offered to book their accommodation and suggested we could all travel together. This was logical but so much for my stipulation that people would arrange their accommodation and transport.

The sleeping arrangements for camping had been discussed in the plan of action. We bought a tent with this situation in mind and opted for a three-man tent, well two-woman one-man tent to be precise, and Carl had a one-man home. I think a few people struggled to comprehend our camping carry on, me happy to have another woman sharing our tent, Anita's husband not there, and then Carl a divorced man in his little tent. However, those who needed to agree to the arrangements were more than happy.

We were ready and looking forward to the first weekend in March, when only days before we were due to leave, I developed a chest infection. I'd been off work, a rarity in itself, but felt that I had to return if I was planning on Munro bagging. The train was 25 minutes away from Leeds when I started to feel decidedly ill. I desperately needed some fresh air so, squeezing past the standing passengers, I made my way to the end of the carriage where the guard was. 'You look dreadful luv, are you OK?' was a distant echo as I started to sway, aware of shapes where people once stood. The guard couldn't have been kinder and was eager to arrange for an ambulance to meet the train. Normality seemed to resume so I kindly, but firmly, refused his offer. That would scupper the visit to Scotland.

The work idea was abandoned as I went home to bed, dosed myself with pills and potions and prayed I would be OK the following morning. The possibility of the other three going but not me was a huge incentive. I felt sure Dave wouldn't abandon me, but how could I miss a trip of MY challenge … no thank you. Of course, had it just been the two of us we could have easily changed our plans, but we had Anita and Carl to consider. The idea of going places without a care in the world was trickier than I first imagined.

* * *

On 2nd March we arrived in Crianlarich, parked up and walked to Coire Earb near the River Falloch and where Dave wanted to camp. When it came to cooking and fetching water, Anita teamed up with Carl. Dave instructed me what to do as of course the relationship between me and camping procedures was minimal. As I didn't have a clue how to erect a tent, not knowing which poles went where, Dave found it less hassle to do that himself and sent me to collect water. Even that seemed easier said than done and I would still like to know if it's possible to collect freezing cold water without immersing one's hand in the water – the pain of the cold!

I then went to find a suitable toilet area with the idea of digging in readiness. After the business of not eating enough spicy bean casserole in the snowhole, I knew I had to eat sufficiently to keep my energy levels up. Advanced digging seemed like a good idea; that was until the hole was required and I couldn't find the damn spot. Frantic digging ensued, but I would not be beaten for future visits so a makeshift flag marked the spot. Wild camping and Irritable Bowel Syndrome are not the best of companions.

I managed to grab some sleep even though I was propped up against my rucksack, coughing, sneezing and sweating although the temperature was close to freezing. I was pig in the middle and slept the opposite way round with my head at the foot which gave everyone plenty of space. I'm not sure how well the others slept, but this was going to test our friendship from the start.

The following day we bagged An Caisteal and Beinn a'Chroin. There had been talk of including Beinn Chabhair, but with snow underfoot, the mist drifting in and out and with me plodding on behind feeling like death warmed up, that idea was dismissed.

Next day was the turn of Beinn Tulaichean and Cruach Ardrain and the bonus of an evening at a B&B. In the past, the furnishings and colour schemes of such establishments had been known to clinch a booking. However, that particular evening, just the sight of a bed AND en suite bathroom were appreciated all the more for having roughed it for a couple of nights. I never noticed whether the curtains and carpets matched.

We had a lovely meal at the Ben More Lodge of red wine and steak with all the trimmings and of course, Carl's steak was larger than ours. We had the added entertainment of one of the locals telling us various tales about the mountain, Ben More. The most enthralling story was about a body found in a tent years after the poor person had gone missing. Whether it was true or not, it sounded convincing, I knew my gut instinct about tents was right after all.

CHAPTER 4

Crabby on Klibreck and Moody Mhic Choinnich

April 2013

Prior to the challenge being conceived, we had booked a rather special holiday where relaxation was on the agenda. I had found a beautiful cottage on the Isle of Lewis overlooking a sandy bay, the outside akin to a Teletubby house yet the interior could have easily featured in some home design magazine. We could just about afford it at the end of March and chose to ignore the fact that our close friends, Diane and Glynn, had experienced the Outer Hebrides when it rained every day for a week with gale force winds thrown in for good measure. That would have been far from perfect for us, but our poor friends were sun worshippers. Our luck was in, we had glorious weather and the dream I had envisaged materialised. Some friends had joined us and we were all treated to an aerial display by four golden eagles. It was an ideal opportunity to make the most of being a long way north, and since we were returning to Ullapool the four most northerly Munros seemed to beckon.

Anita and Carl were game to drive up and meet us so I made a booking for three nights north of Lairg. The couple who ran the B&B were fantastic. Slightly unusual colour schemes in one or two of the rooms, which I may not have chosen, but who is to say my choice of decor is right? They couldn't have been more helpful and friendly, and had we wanted breakfast at 4.00am it wouldn't have been a problem. This was a far cry from a visit to a beautiful establishment in Pitlochry that normally served breakfast at 8.00am. We had asked if we could eat at 7.30am or 7.45am, but the earliest they could offer was 7.50am, rather petty I would say.

We drove to Inchnadamph with Ben More Assynt and Conival on the list. It started to snow, gently at first and then became heavier, but it all felt rather peaceful and quite therapeutic. I'm sure it wasn't quite as relaxing for Dave as he was chief navigator. Everyone helped to a greater or lesser degree, but the onus was on Dave. I think he preferred it that way and loved his map and compass. We owned a GPS but it was rarely switched on. Dave is a strong believer in traditional methods and doesn't want to become reliant on such devices. I was the one with the least experience. I participated quietly but when three people were huddled round a map, I reckoned a fourth wasn't going to make any difference. The chance of me uttering words of wisdom was unlikely, although my gut instinct often turned out to be correct when we were in the mountains. Both Munros were bagged and we returned to the car to find the roads were rapidly changing from black to white. This was quite a change from our shorts and T-shirt week back on Lewis.

* * *

The following day was to be Ben Klibreck and Ben Hope, and the start of a steep learning curve. The more you learn the more you realise you know very little. I have no idea why we thought both mountains were possible on the same day, in winter conditions. Klibreck was covered in snow, which should have been a big enough hint in itself, plus the fact that Ben Hope entailed returning to the car and driving further north to start that mountain.

Sadly, I was not in a positive mood which stemmed from Dave having been talking about two possible routes for Klibreck. There was a longer but possibly easier route that had the luxury of a bridge over the river Vagastie … put my name down. The route everyone else seemed happy with was a shorter more direct route, steeper and without a bridge. Majority rule won. I was pathetic crossing the river, with my mind dreaming about a bridge just a little way downstream. This was followed by the delights of trudging through boggy ground hidden by the snow. Sometimes you could get away with it then the next step you were calf deep in mud.

By the time we started to climb the western flank, heading onto the A'Chioch ridge, I had a serious sense of humour failure. Intimate encounters with heather poking through the snow had broken the camel's back and we had only been going an hour. Cursing and swearing seemed to make no difference whatsoever to my predicament so when Dave glanced back and told me to shut up and get on with it he only succeeded in fuelling the flames. After performing a variety of gesticulations behind Dave's back, I felt better.

Carl was further away having chosen a slightly more difficult angle to attack the slope. This also irritated me, as surely we should be working as a team. What was he trying to prove? This was my challenge. Oh dear, perhaps it was a case of "Miss Jealous Pants". However, as I regained composure, I could see the mountain side steepening and even from a distance the snow appeared to be a solid mass of white. We stopped to put our crampons on and get the ice axes out. I knew what to do but my legs had gone to jelly. With some coaxing from Dave and Anita, and having given myself a good talking-to, we continued.

We reached the summit of Klibreck with every rock covered in ice and the wind cutting like a knife, but at least I was smiling. It was a quick about turn, retracing our steps until we returned to the point where we had joined the ridge. Only then did I realise that Dave was planning on going down the way we had come up. No panic, I was calm and in control of myself. Quite simple, I was not going down there, end of story, and it was not open to debate. We had a civilised discussion and Dave actually listened to what I had to say. I raised various points we had been taught back in February, in particular the use of an escape route even if it is further. I could see a route that looked rather more enticing with an easier angled slope. Dave agreed and after tweaking it a little as we went, with me even leading part of the way, we were safely down. My positive head had returned, so no more trailing on behind, and I was happy I had helped in some small way. The "dreadful" burn we needed to re-cross was insignificant. What a difference a few hours can make to one's mental well-being.

As the ridiculous notion of Ben Hope had to be aborted, a serious rethink was required. We were due to drive home the following day but because Ben Hope is the most northerly Munro it couldn't be efficiently combined with a future trip. All agreed the drive home would be delayed by a few hours and the following morning Ben Hope would be visited. Carl was all for a 4.00am breakfast. I suggested 7.00am, but I think we compromised on 5.30am.

The temperature was well below zero with a chilling wind blowing from the north, but we enjoyed brilliant sunshine and clear blue skies. We had read varying descriptions about the view from this mountain, some quite disparaging, but as we reached the summit the isolation was breathtakingly beautiful. The thought of a 450-mile drive ahead of us didn't matter a jiff.

May 2013

Three months, three visits and nine Munros in the bag were better than none, but we needed to be making better headway. Perhaps a forthcoming visit to Skye for a whole week would help, and even if the quantity wasn't there, the quality would compensate. While the In Pinn is the most difficult Munro, there are several more on Skye that come into the knee-knocking, heart-stopping category. The sooner I could climb them, the sooner I could rest easy in my bed.

Once again it was a week we had booked prior to the campaign. Anita, Carl and our sun-loving friends, Diane and Glynn, would be joining us as we returned to a favourite cottage near Carbost. We had often experienced good weather in May, hence Diane and Glynn's presence. I'd persuaded them to join us and suggested they could relax and sit in the sun while we were in the mountains. Unfortunately, 2013 was an exception as we were greeted to the sight of the Cuillin in full winter conditions.

We ventured into Coire Lagan to have a closer inspection at Sgurr Mhic Choinnich, fooling ourselves that the snow and ice may have bypassed this mountain; yes, we were clutching at straws! A mountain guide was coming down who was most helpful and suggested we could go a little further. However, he had decided it was unsuitable for his group due to verglas (a type of ice). Well, at least we must have appeared to be proficient.

Looking was quite sufficient to confirm that retreat was the wisest option, and I would have turned round there and then, but the men wanted to be men and wanted to see how far they could get – the answer was not very far. Even if we'd had a rope there was not a cat in hell's chance we women would have gone any further. Carrying a rope was one piece of kit that was rather new to us and something that would be necessary for certain future trips. Dave had previously climbed this mountain on a gloriously sunny day and told me it was straightforward. My verdict on this matter will come somewhat later.

Just looking at Mhic Choinnich, or rather what I could see of it, made me anxious, a totally different feeling to when I was on the Forcan Ridge when the sun was shining. Part of "Mhic's" armour was shrouded in mist with the occasional glimpse of icicles hanging like tendrils from the murky rock face. "He" would not be taking any prisoners that day, and if a mountain could be in a bad mood I reckon this was a good example.

As all the least difficult Munros on Skye had already been climbed on previous visits, there wouldn't be any more bagging on the Cuillin Ridge that week. The only option was to pop across to the mainland and find something more manageable. With the best will in the world, my skills and certainly my confidence didn't extend to tackling the mountains on Skye in such conditions. Diane and Glynn couldn't comprehend why we would go all the way to Skye to then drive back to the mainland. They also doubted our previous tales of fantastic weather on Skye, and Glynn vowed he would be reverting to holidays abroad.

In seven days the Munro tally increased by two, meaning that our average was going from bad to worse. Even the two we conquered didn't come easily, and they were both in the balance until the last moment due to whiteouts and gales. On Creag a'Mhaim in Glen Shiel we met two chaps who had turned back 500ft from the summit after being pebble-dashed by horizontal hail. We made it thanks to our goggles, and luckily my negative stance on Klibreck had been superseded by out-and-out determination.

The other mountain was Ciste Dhubh. It was hard work with blizzards and high winds to contend with, but I was more than happy. Dave and Carl had planned to climb Pinnacle Ridge (on Skye) with Martin, but it had been postponed. This was a stroke of luck for Anita and me as we had intended to bag Ciste Dhubh on our own. Without the men we would have no choice other than to abandon the idea because of the conditions.

As we drove back through snow, partially flooded roads, torrential rain and the car being buffeted by the wind, I was still smiling – and it was me who was negotiating the road conditions. Elton John was our background entertainment and certain tracks still remind me of that enjoyable wintry day in May.

Sue on the second, easier pitch on the Pinn.

Not the weather we'd hoped for!

Smiling faces and mission accomplished with our guide Martin Moran.

Approaching the top of the snow gully.

The start of the Forcan Ridge. Photo: Martin Moran.

Alpine conditions on the Forcan Ridge.

The snow cave. Carl happily shovelling snow.

Summit of Sgurr na Sgine. 50th Munro but the first of the challenge.
L to R. Anita, Sue, Dave and Martin

Heading for the A'Chioch ridge leading to Ben Klibreck.

View from the summit of Ben Hope.

Our home in the breezy bealach on the Seana Bhraigh trip.

The Ring of Steall-An Gearanach.

The wise man in his shelter on the summit of Glas Maol.

Late afternoon sunshine and snow showers after visiting An Socach.

Looking towards Sgurr Mhic Choinnich in relatively acceptable weather conditions.

Modelling the sock strategy on Sgurr Mhic Choinnich.

Summit of A'Ghreadaidh and Anita's love of rock-hugging.

View towards Loch Coruisk from the summit of A'Mhadaidh.

Thankfully; farewell to An Dorus.

Coastguard rescue helicopter hovering near Sgurr Dearg.

CHAPTER 5

FRIED OR FROZEN

July 2013

We were taking every opportunity to head north so it was a return to wild camping for the two of us, plus Anita. Seven months into the challenge and Anita had been bitten by the Munro bug. From hoping to join us on some of our trips, Anita had wholeheartedly committed herself to Munro bagging without causing too many problems at home. Her husband, a golfing fanatic, had possibly seen the potential of being "home alone". Perhaps additional golfing trips with his friends would help while away the lonely hours. He commented one day, 'Shame there's ONLY 282 Munros'.

The weather forecast was looking good. However, it was at the height of the midge season which was not ideal. But then a challenge meant exactly that in whatever format the challenge took. Sadly, the weather had gone overboard on the promise of sunshine when it was announced on the radio that 29°C had been recorded in Inverness. Perhaps the majority of people welcomed the news, but my heart sank. I was desperately clinging onto the hope that a breeze would be my saviour. Anita would be fine; her thermostat was far more compatible with hot weather.

The West Highlands and Loch Mullardoch was the destination with Carn nan Gobhar, Sgurr na Lapaich, An Riabhachan and An Socach in mind. Camping seemed the obvious choice as all four Munros are remote and it helped the bank balance. The plan was to have three nights camping and climb the mountains over two days. Climbing all four in one day seemed a little too much and yet split over two days appeared rather wasteful. Do remember, I'm talking about the first year of the challenge and what seemed like a long day in year one would be a far cry from the meaning of a long day in year three.

We parked near the dam of Loch Mullardoch with the faintest of breezes blowing as we opened the car doors. With the sun beating down we headed for some shade while getting our boots on, and this was late afternoon. The sun shimmered on the loch, with mountains in every direction paying homage to the great orange ball in the sky. There was a small boat bobbing up and down in the water – what a picturesque setting.

The Allt Taige was to be the proposed pitch for the next few nights. I was getting hot even though I had risked wearing shorts. Do you cover up because of the midges but overheat, or do you expose some flesh and risk making the midges lives so much easier when in search of a meal?

We had gained a little height, a breeze was blowing and everything was looking rosy. We started to unpack and I assumed my water bearer duties, which was most enjoyable in this idyllic setting. I even came across a potential skinny dipping pool – perhaps something to enjoy later, although I doubted we would feel at ease doffing off in front of someone we knew.

Dave and I once sampled the delights of a nudist beach in Norfolk. Initially, there were the usual hang ups and feeling self-conscious, but after a while it felt rather pleasant. Everything was fine until a charming gentleman walked up to talk to us. He was standing and I was sitting down which, thankfully, concealed various parts of my anatomy that had seen better days. However, I quickly realised that had I been standing up I would have benefited by being face to face. How can you have a meaningful conversation when your only thought is, 'remember to keep looking upwards'? He knew we were newcomers to this sport, the patchy tans being one giveaway, but he pointed out that we were sitting in the gay section. I thought it was very kind of him to come across and inform us. Dave thought he was just showing off. Back to Scotland.

We had been there about an hour when the breeze disappeared and in its place a cloud of midges took over. I quickly exchanged my shorts for a pair of trousers and put a thin pair of gloves on. The three of us had our midge nets on faster than you could say Deet. They must be one of the most unflattering items of headgear you can wear, but until you've been bombarded by midges, don't knock it. Even trying to drink a cup of tea without a scum of drowned midges was an art. Anita was doing her best to fish them out but I was impatient so drank my tea, dead midges and all. Dave cooked a meal with a midge topping nicely developing on it.

A different plan of action was required and the least time we spent camping would be a bonus. So we agreed that the four Munros would be done in one day and accepted that it would be a long haul. I had a hunch that this escapade was going to feel as though time had stood still. Dave was doing his best to assure me that midges went to bed at night. The jury is still out on that one, but if that was the case our midges were stop-outs. Despite my loathing of these creatures, I had an urge to sleep outside to observe the moon and stars. In any case, it was hot in the tent and midges had managed to creep in. I'd been told to keep the tent zipped up, but in order to access anything, surely I had to unzip it? Dave chose to join me outside and Anita had the tent to herself. I still wore my midge net, but it was wonderful, watching the stars with the mountains silhouetted by the moon.

* * *

I woke to a horde of midges inches from my face, with only the midge net between me and them and with the sun's orange face gently frying me. Where to have a pee was the next problem. Although I had drenched myself in various insect repellents I knew they were out to get me. Our breakfast was porridge with a side helping of black blobs, and because midges like their prey to be still, I was constantly walking round in circles trying to eat.

By the time we started to walk, I was hot and bothered from both the heat and the critters, and the only thing that spurred me on was the hope of cooler climes once we climbed higher. My hopes weren't in vain and occasionally there would be a tiny patch of snow tucked away. I became eagle eyed at spotting this white nectar. A handful of snow stuffed in my hat, resulting in ice cold meltwater dripping down my neck was ecstasy.

All four Munros were gems, amidst hundreds of mountains as far as the eye could see, with hardly a trace of civilisation. There had been fantastic views on previous visits to Scotland but this spectacle was breathtaking. Going from one Munro to another was invigorating and the woes of the previous evening had vanished into thin air. I was a little miffed when we met three people and their dog on An Riabhachan (well, the dog was fine). I let Dave and Anita do the "pass the time of day" ritual while I chatted to the dog. Happily, we were going in the opposite direction to them. In the short space of time we'd been Munro bagging I had developed a dislike for sharing the mountains with others. I would willingly speak but avoided lengthy discussions, particularly if they were young, female and a darn sight fitter than me.

On completing the four mountains I had to face up to it being a long walk back to the tent. No problem, or so I thought. But I'm afraid the mind or rather the memory plays tricks with you. A perfect day, with spectacular views and not a midge in sight all made for a rather idyllic bubble. We descended towards the loch and reached a rather rough path. Admittedly, the path was less than ideal but I knew that I was on the homeward stretch. The path was never-ending and the idyllic bubble was fast disappearing. By now my dear little friends the midges had returned, and brought their mates along with them, horseflies/cleggs, call them what you will.

We stopped by the loch-side for a very quick break, the rucksack came off and I had the last swig of water – 3.5 litres of fluid had passed my lips that day. Foolishly, I enquired how much further it was and foolishly, Dave told the truth. The answer was not what I wanted to hear. Chuntering didn't help, but just for good measure I kicked my rucksack with great gusto which brought instant relief. Well, for all of 30 seconds which was as long as it took me to realise that I had just kicked my midge spray thus making it inoperable. I knew exactly what Dave was thinking, but regrettably he also uttered his thoughts. Another rant was my reply. Of course I knew that I'd been childish to kick it and of course I knew that I had to get on with it. Jealousy reared its ugly head as Dave and Anita walked on. I once read that jealousy is a futile emotion. Perhaps so, but I know that it screws you up if unchecked. Why could Dave and Anita control their frustrations when I could not? The more they "behaved", the more I would get annoyed. If only they would throw a wobbly now and then, I would feel so much better.

I walked some distance behind which benefited everyone. But 30 minutes later I felt ill, silence descended, and I ground to a halt no longer caring about the insects feasting on me. Dave and Anita came to my aid which I was embarrassingly grateful for, and we finally reached the tent after an agonising uphill climb to our home. Not even Dave, who enjoys his food nearly as much as Carl, could be bothered cooking, and so we ate the remaining sandwiches. The skinny dipping pool idea was dismissed; the midges had beaten us to it.

I slept outside on my own. This was not due to my earlier outburst but because Dave had decided the night before he wanted to be inside.

Some may think this situation was even more absurd than three in a tent. I was outside while Dave and Anita were inside the tent. Anita was in her sleeping bag with her midge net on, with gloves on and smelling of Deet, hardly the Ann Summers look! It was therapeutic in the open air, again gazing at the stars, and although I was shattered and a tad grumpy, I was enjoying this Munro lark and I knew that the mountains and I could become great friends. I may have been alone but I certainly wasn't lonely.

Dawn broke and hooray, we were packing up and heading back to the car – forget breakfast. The long day had saved us 24 hours of yet more hot weather and midges. Dave and I were shocked when Anita suggested that we could perhaps utilise the extra day we had gained and head somewhere else. Dave hastily announced that we had done what we had set out to achieve and in the circumstances, namely the hot weather, we would be heading home. Oh for some cold weather.

March 2014

Out of the midge season and no scorching temperatures to contend with, I was in a very positive frame of mind as we drove to Inverlael, south of Ullapool. Perhaps this wild camping adventure would be more enjoyable. Dave and I had two Munros in the area that still required bagging, Am Faochagach and the extremely remote Seana Bhraigh. We had promised Anita that after our challenge was complete, we would return with her to "mop up" any mountains that she still needed to visit. However, Dave had found a route that would not only encompass our two mountains, but also four additional Munros for Anita's benefit.

The idea was to camp at the bealach between Beinn Dearg and Meall nan Ceapraichean. (A bealach is the same as a col which means a gap or a pass between two peaks or ridges.) The plan of action was:

Saturday – Drive to Inverlael (380 miles), walk up to the bealach, Dave and I pitch the tent while Anita popped up Beinn Dearg.

Sunday – Meall nan Ceapraichean, Eididh nan Clach Geala, Seana Bhraigh, back to the tent.

Monday – Cona' Mheall and Am Faochagach, back to the tent, pack and walk back to the car.

Monday evening – One night B&B in Ullapool.

Tuesday – Drive home.

The journey to Inverlael was a fast but easy relaxing drive. It was a lovely day and the full winter gear we had packed was beginning to feel unnecessary. Dave and I were in short sleeves; surely to goodness I wouldn't overheat in March. However, snow-capped mountains could be seen in the direction we were heading so the weighty rucksacks on our backs wouldn't be in vain. All three of us were in good spirits as we walked through the forest before heading out onto open land. Two contrasting environments, the comforting green of the forest cocoon and the soothing sound of water in the nearby burns, but ahead of us lay the rugged mountains with their snow-covered peaks twinkling in the sun.

On reaching the snowline the pace slowed. The snow was fairly deep, not particularly firm, and the final hour had become tiresome. We had gained considerable height and reached the bealach at 2,880ft (877metres) just as the sun began to set and an uncomfortably strong wind appeared from nowhere.

The choice of where to pitch the tent was akin to the devil and the deep. Shelter from the wind but have boulders for a mattress or a relatively soft piece of ground but in the wind? The softer option was chosen with the slightest advantage of a partially frozen stream close at hand. Head-torches were the next requirement as daylight had all but disappeared and the idea of a simple hop up Beinn Dearg for Anita had long since gone out of the window.

I was still in good spirits and still in adventure mode. Dave was keen to pitch the tent as quickly as possible which became increasingly difficult in the wind and dark. Anita and I remained calm and did as Dave instructed, even though it felt more like flying a kite. With hindsight, we wondered why we had chosen a bealach for our home when they're notorious for funnelling the wind; you live and learn.

The idea of a hot meal had been dismissed, so sandwiches, chocolate and a hot drink became the revised menu. However, there was the small issue of me and my sleep-mat. I had an Exped 7 Downmat, excellent comfort with first-rate insulating properties due to the down filling but equally essential, the air cushion once inflated. Could I hell as like get the thing inflated, and while I was inside the tent wrestling with my upmarket lilo, Dave and Anita were stuck outside in the elements. Things were taking a downward spiral as feathers floated about the tent and on closer inspection of the mat, I discovered a hole the size of a fifty pence piece.

Many moons ago there had been problems with mice in our loft and that was where the camping gear was stored. To think we had agreed on using a humane mouse trap to give the poor little dears a second chance. At nigh on 3,000ft high, in the snow and with a howling wind, my animal loving nature was quickly vanishing. The thought of a family of mice snuggled up in a down-filled nest while I had a sleep-mat with sod all insulation was a hard pill to swallow. Another lesson to be learned; check your gear beforehand.

A good friend and work colleague of mine, Richard, often used the expression 'bloody marvellous' but more often than not it would imply quite the contrary. The tone in his voice remained the same and it took a trained eye to decipher the very subtle changes in his body language before you knew what he actually meant. I'm afraid there was no question of how I meant it. I would need far more training from the expert to be as subtle as Richard.

By some miracle I remained calm, accepted that nothing could be done about it (I hadn't brought the repair kit with me) and I was going to be less than comfortable. Looking on the bright side, we were minus midges and I wasn't going to overheat. Rather than sleeping the opposite way round to Dave and Anita which gave more space, I decided to be the same as them. There was less room but extra warmth.

I could hardly say I was warm in spite of every item of clothing being utilised, placing what I could underneath me. Previously, I had relied on my Downmat to compensate for my TWO-season sleeping bag. When I purchased my sleeping bag I had no intention of making a habit of camping and certainly not in winter conditions. Never mind, I wasn't totally cold and being in the middle I was spared the tent sides flapping in my face … unlike Dave and Anita. We all thought the chances of the tent remaining upright was in the balance even though Dave had used small boulders to help give stability to our home.

How things change from the sublime to the ridiculous. We had been at a 60th birthday celebration the previous weekend enjoying a complimentary stay at a rather upmarket boutique hotel in the Yorkshire Dales. Slippers and fluffy dressing gowns were supplied. But now I was wide awake listening to what sounded like a howling gale with not a fluffy dressing gown in sight.

* * *

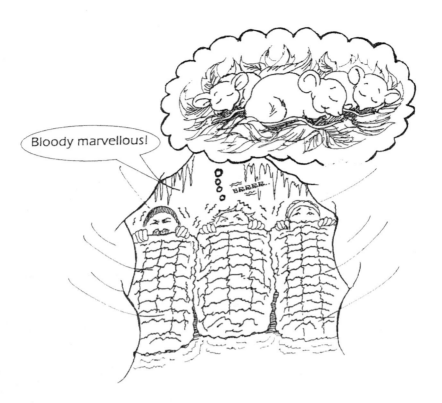

The morning finally came and although blustery, it was calm enough for Dave to make some porridge while Anita and I chipped away at the ice to reach the stream trickling below. It was excellent to have hot food but the consistency was in keeping with cement. With my best diplomatic hat on I suggested "we" could use a little more liquid next time. Oh for a bacon sandwich. Rucksacks were packed and the tent secured with a few more boulders before we headed for Meall nan Ceapraichean, Eididh nan Clach Geala and the ultimate goal of Seana Bhraigh. The cloud was down but high enough to make Dave's life easier with the navigation.

We trailed our winter gear round with us but didn't require it. Overall, the day was going well, but in fact a bit too well. We had one break and agreed the next stop wouldn't be until we reached the summit of Seana Bhraigh. Unfortunately, it was significantly further than we had envisaged. I did my best to stay focused and positive and even Dave was beginning to lag behind, yet nobody seemed to want to suggest a break. Enough was enough. I came to a halt and with hands on hips I announced my name was not Martin Moran or Alan Hinkes, but Sue Pugh, a mere mortal, and I for one was going to have a break. Dave sat down nearly as quickly as me. It was probably only 30 minutes from the summit but that was immaterial.

Now refreshed, the determined approach returned and even the sun appeared from behind the clouds as we reached Seana Bhraigh. The mountains often reminded me that they were the ones in charge and they would call the shots. However, I loved them dearly and the feeling of isolation from the outside world worked wonders for body and soul, far better than any anti-depressant.

Adrenaline would spur me on getting to my goal, but it never worked quite the same on the return leg. The thought of the long journey back to our tent was a sobering affair. Dave perused the map in search of any shortcuts and bless, he found a route that would reduce distance and ascent. We dropped into Coire Gorm avoiding Eididh nan Clach Geala and then evaded Meall nan Ceapraichean by going to the east side of Ceann Garbh and south back to the tent (for those of you into routes). The new itinerary also permitted having a break when we needed one rather than walking ourselves into the ground. Anita would have continued but went with the majority vote. I hadn't realised Anita was still hoping to bag Beinn Dearg, the Munro which had been abandoned the previous evening. When the trip had been mentioned a plan had been devised to incorporate six Munros. Once you have a figure set in your mind, that is what you want to do and anything less is a disappointment. Having said that, while Dave and I had set a time limit to complete all the Munros, Anita hadn't and therefore I couldn't quite understand the urgency. I had presumed it would be left for another visit.

The tent could be seen in the distance, and while it may have been rough and ready it was a welcome sight. Apparently, Beinn Dearg would be climbed before the evening meal although I felt Dave was shattered. It was suggested that I could start preparing the meal while Dave went with Anita to bag the mountain. Anita had kindly offered to go it alone but we knew that wasn't wise with the light now fading and the mountain covered in snow. I was more than happy to stay and take care of the meal. I indulged in the solitude while giving the stew the odd stir and drinking my coffee, which was sufficiently strenuous for me.

* * *

The sun welcomed us the following morning and we set off in good time as the ultimate goal was Am Faochagach. But first we needed to visit Cona' Mheall. It necessitated the odd diversion due to the volume of deep and rather soft snow lurking in numerous nooks and crannies, but its summit was easily reached. Anita and I were busy taking photos while Dave went in search of our proposed descent. He returned but with that look in his eyes that said it all. It was a definite no. A large cornice barred the way, and our only option was to retrace our steps and circumnavigate the issues. Initially, all went well but only to be faced with yet more hazards. Gullies choked with soft snow and steep snowbanks and all appearing far from stable. Sod's law as today we had opted not to carry ice axes and crampons.

We were losing valuable time and "my mountain", Am Faochagach, was fast becoming a pipe dream. All this planning and our second but main goal was fading away. I was not best pleased. Dave saw a way through the maze of obstructions but questioned the time we had left. As a route had been found I was definitely not for turning back, and we had our head-torches. Why are we governed in life by the clock anyway? Says she, the one who set a time limit.

The route we took down to Loch Tuath was beautiful. The sun was high in the sky with the odd fluffy cloud drifting by and the shimmering water spilling over the rocks in the nearby burn. This was one of those precious moments, and although Am Faochagach still seemed far away it didn't matter, we would get there sooner or later. It was an exhilarating yet relaxing walk to the summit. It was hard to imagine the alternative route onto this mountain is described as "a toil of a pleasure" with horrendous bogs to negotiate. Our route was perfect. Sadly, we had to take our leave of the summit and return from whence we came. We had learned our lesson skimping on breaks, so indulged in a leisurely break back at Loch Tuath. The weather was perfect and it seemed a sin to leave such a place in haste.

The relaxation was over and the steady amble at the side of the burn going down became a slog going back up. Dave must have been tired as he asked me to lead, which was most unusual. We arrived back at the tent to find the wind had returned and the tent was no longer upright. We had it all to pack away, then a lengthy walk back to the car and our B&B in Ullapool was expecting us early evening. Reluctantly, I broke my rule and switched my phone on. A brief call was made to the B&B giving a revised

ETA then the phone was promptly switched off. Why would you want to be in the middle of nowhere and still want contact with the outside world? Sorry, but I do not grasp that train of thought.

We set off in the half light and discovered that in the 48 hours from arriving at the bealach, the condition of the snow had altered dramatically. It was now a mushy pulp and the tiny burns which had been barely visible, were now torrents of water. Boots sinking through the snow into icy cold soup, more times than I care to recall, was pushing the determined approach to the limit and yet I was taking it in my stride. My feet may have been far from cosy and warm, but my mind was content. I admit the final hour before we reached the car was a mental battle for all three of us and we walked in complete silence, but I remained at ease with the world.

We arrived at the B&B a tad before 9pm. A most charming couple met us and the rooms were beautifully furnished. Our hosts telephoned a restaurant in Ullapool and arranged a table for us on the proviso we went straightaway. No problem to us as all we wanted was a proper meal and I didn't give a stuff what I looked like. Welcoming staff were there to greet us and although we suggested they placed us away from other diners, (our "eau de bealach" might not be everyone's cup of tea), they insisted that we were treated equally. A splendid meal rounded off a superb experience.

CHAPTER 6

RING THE CHANGES AND RING OF STEALL

September 2013

I'm not sure if it's a female trait personalising inanimate objects but it appears to be a tendency of mine. Our faithful old Ford Mondeo was doing us proud. She was 11 years old and not a minute's bother. Flossie was her name. She knew to pull in at Stirling service station when we were northbound and also knew where I liked to be in the car park. Even Anita would talk to Flossie and offer words of encouragement. On our homeward bound trips Flossie would head to Abington services, perhaps a sign of OCD. But if in doubt, heading for the same cubicle in the ladies loos at the respective rest areas definitely was.

Of course as far as Dave was concerned a car was a piece of metal which got us from A to B but deep down I think he had feelings for Flossie. Perhaps I became more attached as I was the one who would drive. This was through choice as ever since I passed my test at the age of 17 I enjoyed driving and confess I like to be in control.

So in September 2013 Flossie was told she was going away for a week rather than a long weekend. I'd been pondering on efficiency and costs and decided a week in a self-catering property would be far better. It would be more economical and would give more flexibility regarding early breakfasts and late evening meals. The new tactic was mentioned to Anita and Carl and the "sort yourselves out" requisite was abandoned, although it had never got off the ground anyway. It was easy for me to sort everyone's accommodation, although occasionally I did have to gently remind people I was not a travel agent. Dave wanted a bath rather than a shower and Carl preferred a twin or a double. He stayed in a single room that he nicknamed the Harry Potter room – and they say men are easy going! By choosing out of season dates I found many well-appointed properties at reasonable prices and they all had two toilets which was my stipulation. Now who was being picky?

The Munro tally had only been creeping up – or perhaps crawling might be a more accurate description – so we booked a week when there was a good chance to improve our average and bolster morale. We bagged 15 in one week when we visited the Southern Highlands near Loch Tay and the likes of the Ben Lawers range came into this category. It was on this visit I ticked off my 100th. Meall a' Choire Leith was one of four Munros visited that day. It was a little emotional hitting 100 and it crossed my mind, how would the last one feel? Amazing, happy, sad? I hardly dare suggest that it could even be an anti-climax. Only time would answer that question.

Meall nan Tarmachan was the fourth and I was tired but pleased the way the day had gone. That was until we left the summit of Meall nan Tarmachan, when a glimpse of the green-eyed monster came out of hiding. Three young females were heading our way who were all tall, slim and attractive, and appeared fit in every sense of the word. I just about managed to pass the time of day, but Dave's little face lit up. Chat chat chat. Anita and I walked on. A lone athletic female was bad enough, but three of them, all young and attractive, was just too much to take. After Dave managed to prise himself away he harked back to the previous day on An Stuc. We had met two young chaps and it was Anita and I who were more than happy to tarry awhile. Of course, it's one rule for one and one for another and surely he should know that by now.

* * *

A few weeks later we were staying in North Ballachulish and had invited a few of our friends to join us. This particular day was to be the Ring of Steall which consists of four Munros: An Gearanach, Stob Coire a'Chairn, Am Bodach and Sgurr A'Mhaim, with an arête known as Devil's Ridge and a wire bridge thrown in for good measure. The Munros didn't worry me, or the arête, but the thought of a wire bridge which spanned a river gave cause for concern.

My balance has never been a strong point and I had never learned to ride a bicycle. I tried as a child but failed miserably. After landing head first in some rose bushes the idea of two wheels was abandoned at an early age. As you may have gathered, I didn't have a sense of adventure in my younger days. I wish I could ride a bike, but I'd look ridiculous with stabilisers or Dave holding the saddle running by my side at this stage in my life. It was a shame I gave in easily as there are several Munros which necessitate a long walk in when a bicycle would be handy. Unfortunately, when it came to bagging these it was going to be a case of Shanks's pony.

All too soon we arrived at the bridge and I liked the idea even less. The wires you held seemed far too high. Mercifully, the gods must have been looking down on me as the river was sufficiently low and could be crossed without setting foot on the bridge. The group more or less split equally, half taking the high road and the other half the low road. As we waited for those walking the tightrope, I happened to notice a large group of people heading our way. I felt deflated as my selfish side surfaced, not wanting to share the mountains with a horde of people, or even a handful for that matter. Would I need to walk behind them or in front of them in order to create a gap, would they be fast, would they be slow? In an instant everything changed and I sensed a stupid grin appearing on my face. This group were in uniform; they were paratroopers. I was suitably impressed they didn't use the bridge, but admittedly, they waded through the water and didn't look for little rocks to stand on to keep their feet dry. Dave smiled back at me but was quick to comment I had double standards when my usual default setting was to the contrary. Old habits die hard, and I still say a man in uniform is so smart. In the 1970s when casual dress and long hair on men was fashionable, I could rarely find a boyfriend who appealed.

We had another water obstacle to negotiate, but this time I never gave it a second thought. I followed in the footsteps of the Paras, but it was a shame I hadn't bothered with my make-up that day as off they went. I imagined they would be considerably faster than us and that would be the last we saw of them, but not so. We caught them up as they were taking a break. Naturally, it kept a smile on my face, but I was mentally patting myself on the back for walking at a similar pace. Perhaps I was fitter than I first imagined. However, the size of the packs they were carrying, along with everything else, made my 35-litre rucksack look like Barbie's handbag.

We were ahead of them until we stopped for a break. They were cheerful and chatted but it was no good, I had to have a joke with them. I think Dave would have been surprised if I had kept my mouth shut. I asked if they might consider carrying my little rucksack and leave it at the summit for me. Yes, they certainly could, but would I also like a piggy back? I laughed but hastily declined the offer. Perhaps 35 years ago when I was young and single I would have deliberated on my reply. Although I did wonder if a piggy back to the summit of a Munro would be classed as having bagged it.

We were to meet up once more with the lads. I was genuinely intrigued to know just how much weight they were carrying so I asked if I could attempt to lift one of their packs. It didn't move. Dave had a go and while he lifted it a few inches off the ground that was the best he could do. No wonder they were "only" moving at a similar speed to us. I enquired what weight they were carrying and I swear they said between 40 and 50 kilos. Dave didn't believe me and thought I must have misheard, but I think I was right. Fit or what?

We had enjoyed good views but what had started as a brisk breeze developed into a strong wind. The ridge onto An Gearanach proved to be a little challenging. Anita was blown about – being tall and slim was a disadvantage and for once my meagre 5 feet 2 (nearly) and having a little extra ballast had its benefits.

Dave sensed that people were becoming a little worried on the approach to Devil's Ridge. I was wearing my positive head and felt cautiously optimistic. Who said we had to walk it? Perhaps crawling or bottom shuffling may do the trick. Remaining in a totally upright position would have been a little difficult. However, crouching down was all that was required. My luck was in again as I didn't have as far to bob down, so I stopped to take a few photos. This was much to the alarm of Anita directly behind me who wanted to sally forth as quickly as possible.

People were upbeat as we returned to Glen Nevis, and even the men commented on the Paras and wondered where they were and how they were getting on. My thoughts exactly.

CHAPTER 7

WINTER WONDERLAND

February 2014

Glenshee was an area new to me. The aim of 10 possibly 12 Munros was on the agenda, including Mount Keen, the most easterly Munro. Glenshee would be an easy four-hour trip from home with potentially more manageable mountains, and would compensate for it being more or less a certainty we would encounter snow. It was a thought which rather appealed, in spite of passing a road sign stating the snow-gates on the A93 at the Spittal of Glenshee were closed. It was hard to believe as we admired the lush green fields around us with not a snowflake in sight.

We arrived at our cottage at a tiny place called Mains of Soilzarie, a few miles south of the snow-gates, and still there was no snow. What a beautifully appointed property with home-baked bread, fresh eggs and a decanter of malt whisky to welcome us. I was rather too busy sampling a wee dram and admiring the curtain fabric and tasteful furnishings to think about such things as snow-gates. Nevertheless, the mapping head was ultimately donned.

To access the starting point of Creag Leacach and Glas Maol we needed the snow-gates to be open. This was a scenario I hadn't considered weeks earlier when I was busily completing the Munro spreadsheet "Plan of Action" and submitting it to Mr Pugh for approval.

The gates were opened at 9.30am the following morning. Within minutes we met a gritting lorry travelling in the opposite direction and not a minute too soon. The road was treacherous and huge swathes of ice had formed where standing water had frozen overnight. Unfortunately, the ice was often located on bends. If I wasn't fully awake when we set off, now I most certainly was and my driving skills were being put to the test. Dave offered to drive but as usual I declined. If you cannot drive in bad conditions, then why have a driving licence?

The ice was successfully negotiated only to be replaced by snow. Goodness knows what it was like when the gates were closed. The next concern was whether the parking areas alongside the A93 would be accessible. The walls of snow made by the plough must have been in the region of 8ft high – and to think we queried the snow-gate sign! With much relief where we needed to park was clear. Various shades of white and grey were the palette, with low cloud cover and an icy wind blowing. It was the first time I'd worn my balaclava before leaving the car.

Deep unblemished snow was in abundance which was beautiful to admire but a pig to walk in, sapping energy from your legs within minutes. Luckily, we had Dave ahead of us and using his footsteps made it easier for Anita and me. However, with Dave's inside leg measurement of 33 inches and mine 28 inches, if you're old enough to remember the Ministry of Silly Walks sketch from Monty Python, that will give you a fair idea of what it was like to stride out with little legs, nearly as difficult as making your own footprints.

Our progress was slow and it became apparent we weren't going to manage two Munros, as neither energy nor time was on our side. As we trudged on with the summit of Creag Leacach lurking in the distant cloud we came across several mountain hares, and within a short space of time they became part and parcel of the scenery. Beautiful animals with their white winter coats in contrast to their dark ebony eyes. They emphasised how clumsy and ungainly we humans are in their environment. I'm sure they were teasing us with their agility as they effortlessly scampered about the mountain side, paying little attention to us floundering in the snow.

We arrived at our goal, pleased at managing the task, and it was hardly surprising that we hadn't seen or a met a soul. It was a pity we would have to start on our return journey and Glas Maol would be shelved for the time being.

* * *

The next day we could forget about the snow-gates as we were heading to Glen Clova in the opposite direction. It was a normal trunk road until we headed down the glen itself. There was plenty of slush on the single track road but nothing to impede our progress. There's no point listing the names of the Munros that we had planned as we didn't get anywhere near them. We walked or rather attempted to walk on an old drovers' road, a path known as Jock's Road. Thigh-deep snow got the better of us. It was exhausting, but it also concealed serious hazards with huge holes and deep troughs. The snow was too soft to hold any weight and it took several minutes for Dave to be extracted from a deep hollow. Unfortunately, it was time to surrender and wave the white flag. The excitement of the proposed Munros had melted.

On Tuesday, a very subdued threesome found themselves back in the car heading once more to Glen Clova in an attempt to tackle two different Munros: Driesh and Mayar. Dave had looked at the map and with a little bit of luck we stood half a chance of succeeding. The temperature had dropped considerably overnight which would hopefully improve the condition of the snow. I realised that the agenda of 10 or 12 Munros in the week had gone out of the window. What a wonderful start to 2014, our second year. We had arrived Saturday, it was now Tuesday, and we had the measly sum of one under our belts.

After the first section of walking through woods we reached firmer snow, thank heavens, as soft snow nearly always equates to hard work. We were beginning to make good progress with the chances of visiting both mountains looking a strong possibility. And then a wind appeared from nowhere and within minutes we were in a whiteout. Apologies to those who know exactly what a whiteout feels like, but it might be helpful if I can portray an image for those who have not had the pleasure. At the risk of stating the obvious, everything is white. The sky and ground are seamless and establishing whether the ground you are walking on is level or has an incline, only your legs will tell you that. You cannot see ups and downs, but then it's hard to see anything, other than a blanket of nothing. As for the direction you think you've walked, forget that, because by now the brain has been totally disorientated.

Initially, I found it quite unnerving and if it was not for my 100% trust in Dave and his navigational skills with map and compass, I would have been frightened. However, my faith in Dave proved correct and after a while I began to enjoy this white world. Anita and I did whatever we could to help, counting steps, re-checking with Dave and the map, and occasionally switching on the GPS to confirm a grid reference. Anita also drew a smiley face in the snow with an arrow as we would need to retrace our steps at some stage. Dave relied on the compass, although there were signs of the smiley face still showing on the return journey which we pointed out to Dave. He chose to trust his compass – a wise move. For nearly five hours we were in the world of white but both Driesh and Mayar were visited, hooray, and I had thoroughly enjoyed myself.

Mount Keen involved a fairly lengthy drive and so that idea had gone the same way as our original agenda. By now an additional visit would be required to attend to unfinished business and a hastily conceived Plan Z was hatched for the remainder of the week.

An Socach came into play which meant back up the A93 passing through the snow-gates. It's a credit to the respective highways authorities who keep that road open. An Socach went very smoothly, with us only encountering a whiteout lasting a couple of hours. I was more than happy to stroll along, inwardly singing either an Elton John track or one of Neil Diamond's. To the relief of others, I rarely sang out loud, but should I forget then Dave would remind me that I had been asked to leave a church choir when I was in my early twenties. I still say it was nothing to do with my singing abilities, limited as they were. Let us say that we had a difference of opinion.

As we returned from An Socach it was late afternoon and we weren't that far from the car when we finally caught a glimpse of the sun. The sky was slowly changing from milky white to glorious pastel shades of pink and blue. There was the tiniest of snow flurries which sparkled in the shafts of sunlight. I used my ploy of deliberately hanging back in order to walk alone. The testing conditions from earlier in the week were becoming a distant memory and now we were rewarded for our perseverance. Bagging Munros doesn't have to mean purely a tick list as I once thought. It may sound twee, but I whispered a thank you to the mountains before reaching the car.

The forecast was looking good for the following day. That night I struggled to sleep, being eager to be back outside. In view of the favourable forecast we had dared to consider tackling the three Munros of Carn an Tuirc, Cairn of Claise and Glas Maol (take two). If we succeeded it would also take my tally over 141, the halfway mark.

* * *

We set off once more on the A93 with not a cloud in the sky. Flossie was doing us proud as we passed the ski centre packed with swish 4 x 4s. I had definitely got out of the right side of the bed and was raring to go. It seemed the mountains were in a good mood too, perfect conditions, sunshine, consolidated snow and excellent visibility. A good helping of laughter and banter, three Munros here we come. And then the cloud descended. Where it had come from I have no idea, but as we reached the summit of Carn an Tuirc we could see nothing. This meant a return of intense navigation for poor Dave, all the way to our second Munro, Cairn of Claise. We admired beautiful ice sculptures where snow had frozen to rocks or to the odd piece of metal, but those were the only objects that punctured the white blanket.

We reached our second Munro when Dave announced he was fed up of the micro navigation, that his eyes were blurring and if the weather didn't improve he would abandon the idea of the third Munro, Glas Maol. Anita and I looked at one another flabbergasted at this announcement. We were both disappointed, but I knew Anita wasn't in a position to say anything. I did my best to appear kind and considerate but only paying lip service to such expressions as 'I understand' and 'that's fine', knowing I was telling out-and-out porkies. Anita and I were on top form, but then we were not at the helm. This mountain, the one that had been abandoned earlier in the week, was thwarting us.

By some miracle the conditions began to slightly improve and we met some people heading towards us. Dave agreed to press on a little further while I did my best to be "so nice" and offered Dave pieces of chocolate. Yes, of course it was bribery, but I stopped short at offering to carry his rucksack. Within minutes the cloud evaporated as quickly as it had arrived. Number three was back on, yippee!

We may have been able to see but actually finding the summit was proving tricky until we saw a pair of skis upright in the snow. The owner of the skis was found drinking hot tea, sitting in a hole 5ft deep with probably a circumference of a similar measurement. Apparently, he was sitting on the summit that was several feet below him. We had a most enjoyable chat exchanging stories and then I was politely put in my place. I commented that earlier on in the week we had wasted a day in the mountains when we had achieved zero Munros. He replied, 'A day in the mountains is never a waste'. How right he was and I'm sure his comment will stay with me for a very long time.

We walked away with the sun on our backs watching skiers from the Glenshee Ski Centre and a panorama of white mountains spreading for miles. What a magical way to end our week. Our tally of seven Munros was smaller than we had hoped, but the man in the hole put everything into perspective; it really did not matter.

CHAPTER 8

CUILLIN COLLYWOBBLES

May 2014

I usually looked forward to visiting Scotland but May 2014 brought mixed emotions. The four of us were heading back to the Isle of Skye. After the miserable weather of 2013 it was heartening that the long range forecast looked good. Unfortunately, the butterflies in the stomach syndrome had returned. Friends and work colleagues were wishing me well but didn't understand why anyone would be anxious about a "holiday".

Hopefully, the remaining five Munros on the Cuillin Ridge would be bagged. As I mentioned earlier, while none of the five were as difficult as the In Pinn they were still serious enough to have very similar side effects on the body's functions. It wasn't compulsory to complete them in 2014 but the longer the wait, the longer the mental torment. I envied people with the skill and confidence to tackle such mountains without teetering on the brink of a nervous breakdown every time they approached Glen Brittle. Until you've seen the Black Cuillin range in the cold light of day, it's difficult to imagine how daunting they look to a non-climber.

As we drove past the Sligachan Hotel we enjoyed the magnificent sight of the northern end of the Cuillin Ridge with only the odd blob of snow here and there. With some luck the blobs weren't going to jeopardise the task in hand. We could monitor the overall picture of the mountains at any time of the day as the cottage we stayed in had an enviable position of uninterrupted views across Loch Harport and the Cuillin. In normal circumstances this was an enjoyable experience, but on this visit it just served to remind me of the mission ahead and wake the butterflies from their slumbers.

First on the agenda was Sgurr Mhic Choinnich along with Sgurr Alasdair. There was high cloud, it was dry and there was no wind. The mountain weather forecast had mentioned the possibility of an occasional shower, but that was acceptable so it was all systems go. Dave was slightly concerned we might encounter the odd section of hidden snow, so rather than go unprepared, full winter gear along with a rope was packed. We also carried helmets taking heed of what we'd been taught. So everything was packed bar the kitchen sink. On arrival at Glen Brittle car park and seeing another group with tiny rucksacks and not an ice axe or crampon in sight, I did wonder who was right. I presumed they were heading high, but why should I conclude that we were the ones who were wrong? Dave's only comment was on the lines of he didn't care what they had or had not; we were prepared.

We headed into Coire Lagan to the start of An Stac screes that would take us onto the Cuillin Ridge itself and the start of Mhic Choinnich. It didn't seem quite the slog it had been the previous year and the further we went it became obvious the ice axes and crampons wouldn't be required. There was a brief debate as to whether our rucksacks along with the winter gear should be left at the start of the climb. All five Munros that week would involve retracing our steps from the respective summits with all other options being more difficult. It was common practice to leave gear at the base of Mhic Choinnich, although in recent years there had been instances of theft. What a sad state of affairs when I for one regarded the mountains as sanctuary from the malicious outside world. The second consideration was safety. Surely all four of us wouldn't be victims of an accident, and if needs be, someone could return to the rucksacks in an emergency. Anita and I stuffed various items in our pockets including a map, a switched off phone and a bar of chocolate in the unlikely event that both Dave and Carl collapsed in a heap.

The grey black buttress ahead looked anything but inviting. Dave was taking it all in his stride and you'd have thought he was just popping up Pen-y-Ghent in the Yorkshire Dales. Carl had a grin from ear to ear, just loving the environment, while Anita and I were rather more reserved and concealing our enthusiasm extremely well. The Cuillin mountains only look inviting with the sun beaming down on them, but any other configuration and I sense they will seize every opportunity to mentally or physically shake you off.

We made steady progress with Dave in front, Carl bringing up the rear and Anita and I cocooned between them. All was fine until the weather threw a spanner in the works as it started to drizzle and the clag (mist) descended. I felt we were nearly at the summit but visibility was very limited. We arrived at some slightly angled rocks that were sloping away and off the mountain, and had the rocks been dry we probably wouldn't have even noticed this section. Regrettably, the drizzle had sufficiently dampened the rocks, which to us women had given them a slippery sheen. Dave and Carl didn't deny this fact but they appeared to have little problem standing upright. If only we knew how far this dubious section went on – so near and yet so far. Anita was beginning to lose her nerve, while I resembled Polly Parrot, repeating time and again, 'There must be a solution, there must be a solution', at the same time walking round in small circles arms stretched wide, pointing to the heavens in the hope of divine intervention. Lightning bolts were not what I had in mind but I didn't want to retreat until all options had been exhausted.

Carl was given the onerous task of babysitting the parrot and the nervous wreck while Dave went ahead to investigate what was in store. My prayers were answered. Within minutes a voice boomed out, 'Summit's 'ere', and the clag lifted just sufficiently to decipher a figure waving at us.

Within five minutes, Dave was back. After this very short section it was apparently easy going, and we would soon be there. Not only had the mist started to lift but it had also stopped drizzling. Using cracks in the rocks as footholds and with the men's help we could do this. To be on the safe side I decided to use a technique I once used in the Lake District on slimy rocks, namely wearing a pair of socks over my boots. Hard to believe but it does give extra grip. Yes, I would get my spare socks out, except no, that wasn't possible as they were in my rucksack hundreds of feet below. Never mind, the rope would come in handy, except no, that was in Carl's rucksack which had also been left behind. What idiots we were. What was the point of coming prepared then to abandon the said items? Would we ever learn and how embarrassing had we got into difficulties? So needs must. The socks I was wearing would have to be used. I was also wearing some liner socks so they stayed on my feet and my brand new £17.99 pair of socks went over my boots. Anita was wearing just one pair so opted to wear them the conventional way.

Dave aimed for the crest as there were more cracks to use but the crest also provided a form of handrail to hold. This was fine for me, peeping over the crest to a vertical drop that looked to be hundreds of feet below, but not so good for Anita with her dislike of exposure. It occurred to me it would have made a good photograph from the opposite side with just eyes, noses and clenched fists protruding over the apex. The men stuck to us like glue, and if they were concerned they weren't showing it. The tiny cracks we were using as footholds didn't faze them. Success as we reached the summit. We didn't hang about as we knew we had to retrace our steps. The rocks seemed a little drier and before too long we felt comparatively safe. I opted to keep my socks over my boots until I was reunited with my rucksack when we could enjoy a well-earned break and at last, Mhic Choinnich was in the bag. My £17.99 socks were in shreds but they were the most well utilised purchase I had ever made. Dave still insisted he remembered this Munro as straightforward. That was not my interpretation of straightforward, and as for Anita I think she still bears the mental scars from that day.

Surprisingly enough we all agreed we should stick with our plan of also bagging the highest peak on Skye, Sgurr Alasdair. Yes, it was going to make it a long day, but it would be an efficient use of our location. At 3.40pm we descended An Stac screes and headed across to the base of the Great Stone Chute. Poor Anita wasn't having the best of days as she fell at the bottom, but luckily was OK to carry on. The descent and re-ascent was a nuisance, but it was the scree that tested morale. The chute is the daddy of scree runs. It was atrocious, with the rubble varying in size from pebbles to mini boulders all moving beneath your feet, not unlike a mini earthquake. Not just a case of two steps forward and one step back, but quite frequently two steps forward and three steps back with the added possibility of a boulder landing on your feet.

Few words were spoken but various thoughts were floating around in my head – it was all rather surreal. However, there were plus points. We had the place to ourselves, it wasn't raining, it wasn't windy and it wasn't scorching hot. The clag was descending again, but perhaps that was a hidden bonus as we couldn't see how far it was before we reached the top of the Great Stone Chute.

At long last the agony abated and we felt the summit was definitely close enough to leave three out of the four rucksacks and collect them on our return. The final push to the summit of Sgurr Alasdair seemed relatively easy after the fiasco on Mhic Choinnich. A quick photo was taken in the mist and then back to the rucksacks and down the Great Stone Chute.

I have no idea what time we got back to the car but at least we had ticked off two more Munros and could look forward to a relaxing meal back at the cottage. Red wine lifted the spirits and diluted the memories, so perhaps the day hadn't been that bad after all. The maps came out in readiness for the following day and Sgurr Dubh Mor.

* * *

It was sunny and no more carrying ice axes and crampons, and perhaps the shorts might even make an appearance. For some reason I had it in my head that today would be easier, or would it be a case of ignorance is bliss? Parking up at Glen Brittle felt like we'd never been away – not that many hours had passed anyway. The Cuillin looked far more enticing in the morning sunshine with the soothing sound of gentle waves breaking on the shoreline of Glen Brittle beach. This was going to be a good day and we only had one to bag. I knew the walk into Coir' a'Ghrunnda was a considerable distance having been there twice before, but we had perfect conditions today. With far-reaching views out to sea with gannets displaying their skills of diving into the sea to catch their breakfast, did it really matter when we arrived at our destination?

We reached the beautiful loch in Coir' a'Ghrunnda. The approach is deceiving as you think you're there but then find there's another tier to climb and the slightest deviation soon leads to some obstacle to scramble over. Dave chose a slightly longer route thinking it would be easier and would avoid a scramble up the nose of Sgurr Dubh an Da Bheinn. Within minutes we'd lost all sight of the sun as the mist made its usual appearance. We met a couple who'd reached Sgurr Dubh an Da Bheinn but couldn't see a thing so had abandoned the idea of going any further. As they put it, 'What was the point?' This was an opinion which often fuelled heated discussions so we chose to be somewhat ambiguous in our reply and said we would press on a little further.

This intermediate top proved rather awkward with odd patches of soft snow hidden away but invariably on a slope and where you wanted to be. My original idea that this was going to be a good day was altering considerably as we hadn't even reached the main objective. Before reaching the start of the main climb onto Sgurr Dubh Mor we came across a section of tiered rocks, common as muck on the Cuillin. Everyone was clambering up and making good progress except me. By the time we reached the start of the main climb onto the summit I was rapidly losing my nerve and it was my turn to feel decidedly uneasy at what lay ahead. We'd already put our helmets on except Dave who had forgotten his. So, "we" had remembered the rope but not the helmet, hell's teeth!

I would have had words there and then but I would require all the help and reassurance I could get. So I chose to keep my mouth shut – for the moment.

The rope came out. Dave was on a learning curve regarding ropes and the most efficient techniques. While we waited for Dave to coil the rope or whatever you do with ropes, we happened to meet a group of four very nice chaps. I asked them whether they knew if where we were was the easiest possible route, or if there was something "better". Maybe there was a nice little path just round the corner with my name on it, even an escalator – perhaps you can sense the desperation. One of them was a mountain guide who was out with three clients. He confirmed that we were in the correct place and mentioned he would be happy for us to follow them. That sounded like music to my ears except Dave was still busy with the rope. He realised that a 50-metre rope was rather too long and not ideal for the job in hand. At times it resembled a badly behaved boa constrictor with Dave doing his best to tame it. So the mountain guide and his clients disappeared and left the Laurel and Hardy sketch to its own devices. I dread to think what they thought, but perhaps best not to know.

Dave finally had the rope tamed in the nick of time before I had a total nervous breakdown. Anita and I were belayed (i.e. attached to the rope) but naturally Carl was off the lead. Fortunately, the summit wasn't far away and the mist had lifted. And to think I thought this one would be easier. Without hesitation I can confirm that I did not enjoy it, but Anita found it far more desirable than Mhic Choinnich. I'll stick with Mhic, thank you.

Sgurr Dubh Mor had been climbed, but then we had to go all the way back. Oh to sprout wings, especially down Coir' a'Ghrunnda, which by now had become a pain in the backside. Carl and Anita upped the pace and went on ahead of us – it was their turn to prepare the evening meal and we were in separate cars. I'm reluctant to sprint back anyway. It feels as though you're shunning the mountains, wham bam thank you, mam, not interested any more. I think they deserve as much attention on the return journey.

There was a beautiful rainbow and then we watched the sun go down. In its place the stars showed their little faces with the moon a bright silver ball reflecting in the blue-black sea and lighting our way back to the car. Perhaps the day hadn't been that difficult after all – and that was before the wine. Did it really matter it had taken 13 hours before we arrived back at our car? People break records for how quickly they climb Munros. Perhaps we broke the record for how long it could take, but I could live with that.

At 10.45pm we sat down to scrambled eggs, baked beans, toast and red wine. Not even Carl could stomach a large meal at that hour. The only downside of ignoring the clock was the turnaround for the following day. However, I thought it a small price to pay for savouring the magic of the mountains.

* * *

Yes, a very quick turnaround. We would have loved a day off for some respite but we had to grab each potential day of good weather. It was the final two on the menu. Sgurr a'Ghreadaidh and Sgurr a'Mhadaidh. These were the two I feared most as I'd read that the climb out of An Dorus was awkward. It had to be tackled twice, once to get onto Sgurr a'Ghreadaidh and then to access Sgurr a'Mhadaidh. Awkward translated as bloody difficult in my language. Dave had done his best to dissuade me from reading articles and googling photos. An Dorus (The Door) is a narrow and initially steep-sided gap between the two mountains. The more difficult climb is regarded as a Grade 3 scramble – the last grade below a climbing category, but in my book it was climbing.

For those who have encountered horrendous weather on Skye, you may find it hard to believe that yet again the sun was shining. The walk up the side of the Allt a'Choire Ghreadaidh to An Dorus was lovely, easy underfoot, with spectacular scenery and the place to ourselves. I noted several potential wild camping spots for a future visit, but without the black cloud of An Dorus looming large. As we reached An Dorus the Cuillin Collywobbles struck. The legs rapidly turned to jelly accompanied by a sickly feeling in my stomach and suddenly I felt quite cold; I rarely felt cold. Dave was right, I would have been far better not reading about it.

I was making a real dog's dinner of getting into An Dorus let alone climbing out of it. A gin and tonic or any form of alcohol for that matter would have been very handy to calm the nerves and numb the brain. However, none were to hand and so the only option was to pull myself together, get a grip, man up or whatever expression takes your fancy.

At my request we opted to do the more difficult Sgurr a'Ghreadaidh first. Let me get the worst over then hopefully things could only get better. We were well prepared today, nothing had been forgotten, the better behaved rope came out and Dave went up first. Anita and I were belayed individually with Carl hanging back to give help and advice from the rear. It goes without saying that I struggled to find footholds and handholds to my liking, as those which had more rock appeal seemed just out of reach. Carl would indicate where to put my feet only for him to realise I couldn't reach that far. Anita did well with a good five inch advantage in leg length. Yes, I know it's a poor workman who blames his tools, but my tools were too damn short and no doubt some child half my height will have scrambled up there without flinching – bully for them I say!

The air was blue as I tugged and towed but eventually I climbed out of f*****g An Dorus. To add insult to injury some climbers had sprinted up just before us, metaphorically with their hands in their pockets. The clue is probably in the word "climbers". Apparently, I had been the source of entertainment for another group of climbers. They called across expressing their admiration for my vocal enthusiasm and unusual technique. That was the nearest I would get to a compliment, so I grabbed it with both hands. They caught up with us, but then that was no surprise, and assured me I only lacked confidence. They couldn't get their wives anywhere near such terrain. How kind, but I think I lacked a darn sight more than confidence. I could picture myself at junior school in a P.E. lesson standing at the bottom of a rope being told to climb it. The teacher may as well have told me to fly to the moon as the outcome was going to be the same.

I was surprised at how long it was before we reached the summit of Sgurr a'Ghreadaidh and how many smaller obstacles we still had to negotiate, but after the Collywobbles earlier on in the day, the determined head had kicked in. I was far more confident and more than happy to be off the lead until we returned to An Dorus when, of course, I was hooked up again. I did much better going down, but then a controlled slide down the rock face onto safe ground could hardly be regarded as climbing. Rather like a sack of spuds being lowered, it worked, but marks for technical merit were probably zero.

Onto Sgurr a'Mhadaidh and the last Munro on the Isle of Skye – yippee! I could hardly say I was confident climbing out of An Dorus once more, but it was less difficult than the first. Once over the initial hurdle, the easy scramble to the summit of Sgurr a'Mhadaidh was enjoyable and the sun was still shining. Glorious views met us at the summit, my fear had gone and I was one happy bunny. I walked about taking photos and feeling rather relaxed. Anita wasn't quite as enthusiastic about the views looking down to Loch Coruisk and remained seated, hugging a rock until it was time to leave.

With Carl's help from below while Dave belayed us, we returned to An Dorus. Poor Carl did that section three times. He went down first then came back part of the way to guide Anita, then when it was my turn he came back again to help me. Dave thought Carl was being far too soft with us, but perhaps Carl knew which side his bread was buttered.

I was happy as I toddled down from An Dorus and left Anita and Dave connected by the rope. Dave pointed out that although the rope was long, it wouldn't stretch back to the car. Anita had become rather attached in more ways than one to the rope and wasn't for parting with her new-found friend.

It was quite weird walking back to the car as I had expected to feel a huge sense of relief now that the Cuillin Ridge was sewn up, but I felt nothing. Perhaps it was delayed reaction … or was it because I had another "date" with the Cuillin ridge and that I would be on my own?

CHAPTER 9

A DATE WITH SGURR DEARG

May 2014

Just Dave and I were staying for a second week on Skye. Dave's 65th birthday present was another adventure with Martin Moran in the shape of the traverse of the Cuillin Ridge. If they succeeded Dave would be Martin's oldest client to accomplish the feat. Although the ridge is only seven miles in length, it can take up to two days for the average person to cross/climb because of the complexity and technical ability involved.

It was totally out of the question for me to even contemplate the traverse but I could be involved in the role as support team. I offered to provide transport and perhaps meet up at some stage, but I should have known better, as Martin came up with a different idea. In addition to providing a taxi service on four wheels, I could also transport water onto Sgurr Dearg just below the In Pinn, bivvy overnight with them and then return with their unwanted camping equipment. This all sounded exciting although I was a little nervous at the role I was to play. I would be walking on the Cuillin on my own and I hadn't bivvied before. What a place for your first time, with the In Pinn as your neighbour, and there I was in my late fifties excited about a "date" with a rock – memories of the old film, "Shirley Valentine".

I was handed the water to carry, all seven litres of it. Neither Dave nor I had considered the volume I would be carrying. I managed to say nothing but inwardly panicked at the weight of the water. And this was of course in addition to my usual gear and a sleeping bag. Obviously, this was the price to pay for joining the adventure so I would have to allow plenty of time to stagger up Sgurr Dearg.

I drove the men round to the idyllic tiny harbour at Elgol where the boat would take them across to Loch Coruisk. Then it was a case of returning to our cottage to empty my rucksack and ponder on how I could fit a mini reservoir in. Three attempts later, with a ruthless attitude on what I could manage without, and success.

I left the cottage early for the drive to Glen Brittle Youth Hostel, allowing more than enough time for the rendezvous, as the last thing I wanted was to be rushing. But in any case that would have been impossible with my own personal water supply in tow. The old heart rate was going nineteen to the dozen for a variety of reasons. I had been entrusted to meet my date on my own and while apprehensive I was quietly confident. The weather was perfect so there should be no route finding issues. Both Dave and Martin were aware that navigation wasn't my strongest point, but on this occasion they seemed sufficiently confident I would find my way onto Sgurr Dearg. Perhaps another back-handed compliment, but one I would accept.

Thank goodness I had allowed ample time. Even taking into consideration the times I had wild camped I felt sure I hadn't carried such weight. Just placing one foot in front of the other became a work of art. God forbid if I fell over; it would be akin to a sheep on its back with its legs in the air, incapable of righting itself. Although it was fairly obvious where I was heading, I kept checking the map if only to identify various landmarks and to give myself much needed practice. The few times when I walked alone I was far more diligent, otherwise I had a bad habit of leaving it to Dave.

Several people were coming down and each time I would stop to pass the time of day and grab the opportunity for a breather. Nearly everyone enquired where I was heading and they were all kind enough to appear suitably impressed, particularly when I pointed out that I had seven litres of water with me. Perhaps Martin didn't regard this feat as a Herculean task but I did. The load made any manoeuvre difficult and the slightest scrambly bits required much deliberation.

As I was plodding along I happened to notice a less than youthful lady in the distance. She had ground to a halt but appeared to be looking in my direction. As I reached her she asked how far I was going. She had tried to go higher but had been too nervous to continue and consequently turned back. The lady had tried to persuade her husband to join her, but he was having none of it and was back in the car. We chatted a while and then she asked if she could follow me because I appeared to know what I was doing. How looks can be deceiving – I think it was the helmet that did it! I stressed that she would need to return on her own, it was at her own risk, and emphasised that I was certainly not an expert by any stretch of the imagination.

We arrived at some easy scrambling, the place where she had turned back. I found a way through and she followed. I remembered what Dave had always preached: never go up anything you cannot get down and vice versa. We went a little further and arrived at a section she was very unsure of. Once again I pointed out that although I could help her going up, she would have to be capable of making her own way back. She wondered if she could return via An Stac screes, but I quickly replied in the negative, bearing in mind our whereabouts. She made the sensible decision to turn back, but seemed delighted I had "guided" her and was thrilled when I pointed out the top of the In Pinn peeping over the horizon. The lady may have been delighted, but so was I. It had done a lot for my confidence and self-esteem, and perhaps I did know just a little more than I first thought.

I was under no illusions of grandeur as I negotiated the last scramble near the top of the ridge and was relieved to meet up with my old friend the In Pinn. I was rather early but that was immaterial as I would occupy myself one way or another. As I arrived four young people passed me. They were heading back down and so I watched them for a while. How strange, as where I had come up they went down the opposite side. I wasn't aware of any other route but concluded that they knew better than me and perhaps they were climbers and they were on a climbing route.

How attitudes change. I now regarded the In Pinn as a welcome sight. I doubt many people have a pin-up on their desk of a lump of rock – Poldark perhaps, but not the In Pinn. However, Poldark standing on top of the In Pinn could make for a knee-trembling combination. My apologies as the realms of fantasy take over.

Slowly but surely the mountain emptied. What a heavenly feeling to be on the Cuillin with a panorama of mountains and sea in near perfect weather conditions, and all the more special because I was alone. Admittedly, there was comfort in the knowledge that Dave and Martin would be joining me in the not too distant future. The thought of hours on my own up there could have been a little intimidating.

I'd been watching the Coastguard helicopter circling Sgurr Alasdair then he would come closer to Sgurr Dearg and fly off again. An hour had passed and I'd run out of conversation with myself so I wondered whether to listen to some music. It seemed I was contradicting the essence of solitude, but as the music was through earplugs I felt I would not offend the mountains. Wow, it enhanced the moment and very quickly I was living in a very special bubble.

Neil Diamond started the ball rolling with a less well-known track of his, "Be". I'd hardly taken much notice of the lyrics before. Then it was the turn of Elton John. "There's something about the way you look tonight". The music and the mountains were a powerful and emotional duo. I was so happy, but silently the tears began to fall. I looked up at the Inaccessible Pinnacle through a watery blur. It had been my foe for years, but at that moment it was my friend. There was this fin of rock that had opened the door to a very special world, and if I never managed to climb another Munro, my life had already been enriched.

It occurred to me that Dave and Martin would appear before long and how embarrassing if they found me in such a state; most men struggle to deal with tears at the best of times. So a change of tempo in the music was hastily selected and it was the turn of the ex-Abba blonde, Agnetha. A few tracks were a tad melancholy but overall it was good music to have a dance to. There I was jigging and singing away to the In Pinn in my own little world. Dave would cringe at my choice of music as Jimi Hendrix would be far more to his liking. But I was on my own so would do just as I pleased. Sure enough, as I saw Dave and Martin at the base of the In Pinn the music was abandoned and I nonchalantly strolled about with a relaxed, cool as a cucumber appearance. Little did they know what I had been up to.

I wandered a little further then happened to turn round to be taken aback at the sight of a man waving at me. I'd no idea where he'd come from but he was a fair way below. I waved back as I didn't want to appear unfriendly. Then my heart missed a beat as I heard him shout, 'Help'. Was this really happening? He shouted again, this time, 'My friend has broken her leg'. The words coming out of my mouth, 'No problem, I'll come down' didn't match the thoughts whizzing round in my head. This would have been serious on a normal mountain, but why did it have to be on the Black Cuillin of all places? I started to collect some gear together, but I was worried where the casualty might be. I was at my limit of the terrain where I felt safe, but the accident spot could be worse. If I wasn't careful I could be another casualty. But I couldn't abandon the poor man and his friend.

Eureka! The old brain cells woke from their bubble slumbers. Of course, the solution was at the end of a rope. Martin was preparing the rope for him and Dave to abseil off the Pinn so I shouted back at the man that I'd send a mountain guide to their aid and help would be with them within minutes. He seemed happy with that and then I shouted up to Martin to tell him what was happening. Once again life turned on a sixpence. I'd been in the most amazing serene bubble of bliss and tranquility and then bang, I was in the midst of a mountain rescue. But then that is the mountains for you.

I concluded that the helicopter was looking for these people. On his next circuit I would try to attract his attention and point him in the right direction. My mind flashed back to the film, "The Railway Children", when a young Jenny Agutter took off her red petticoat to flag the train down. Obviously, I wasn't wearing a petticoat, red or any other colour for that matter. However, I was wearing a brightly coloured top under my jacket. So the jacket came off and I proceeded to mimic a windmill in overdrive, pointing in the direction of the incident. No idea if it helped but they seemed to head in the right direction, but more than likely a coincidence.

I felt a little guilty as I wasn't taking much notice of Dave abseiling off the Pinn because of the drama unfolding, so he only received a passing glance. Once Dave and Martin were down, Dave and I were instructed to make a bivvy area and put the kettle on while Martin and his rope headed in the direction of the incident. How come his rope didn't resemble a badly behaved snake?

We watched the helicopter hovering for long enough, and then the winchman was lowered. Being winched into a helicopter had always appealed to me, but not in an emergency, so unfortunately that idea would also be filed under realms of fantasy. I busied myself making improvements to our bivvy site while Dave rested. It was the first time I'd seen him utterly shattered; the day's climbing in humid conditions had taken its toll. I was beginning to wonder if age was going to prove too much of an issue for Dave to succeed.

It must have been nearly three hours before Martin returned. He had teamed up with the Skye Mountain Rescue guys on what had been a difficult rescue. The group of young people I'd seen earlier were the group in trouble. They were in a very unstable gully when a huge lump of rock had been dislodged and trapped the girl's leg. They were unsure of their location hence the helicopter circling for quite some time before they found them.

At near enough 11pm we had our meal and settled down for the night. It felt very special watching the stars, with not a sound to be heard and the In Pinn looking down on me. I slept well before an alarm beeped at 5.30am. As we ate breakfast I noticed two or three more bodies appearing from behind various rocks. Apparently, other people had also been up there that night. Oh dear, I hope they didn't hear me singing when I thought I was alone. I accompanied Dave and Martin as far as the bealach Coire na Banachdich where they would continue the traverse and I would head back down to the car.

As I set off I was instructed to stay left, which is what I thought I was doing until Martin yelled at me I needed to be further left. You see, how left is left, at 90°, at 45°? From above it was easier to see the exact line required but once you were on it, the boulders merged into one. I think the men thought it would have been easier for me to go back the way I had come up but I wanted to give the corrie my best shot. The load on my back was just as heavy even though the water had been used, because now I had become a refuse collector, transporting rubbish and the excess camping gear down. My heart was in my mouth as I picked my way through the rocks and slabs with sweat dripping from my forehead as the result of my concentration and nerves. A couple of times I backtracked, scrambling back over boulders when my instinct rang warning bells. It wasn't the easiest of areas to route find and certainly no yellow brick road to follow. After a few deviations I reached safe ground, finally arriving at the path which runs at the side of the Allt Coire na Banachdich.

Just before reaching the car I met some chaps heading towards me, and discovered that one of them was a member of the mountain rescue team which had been out the previous night. He was insistent I should pass his thanks on to Martin for his help along with his rope, which had been invaluable in the rescue. I half joked that Martin had commented that his rope was now somewhat shorter as they were forced to cut it. In view of what Martin had done, he would be more than welcome to a new rope, courtesy of the mountain rescue was the reply.

Later that day I drove to Sligachan to meet Dave and Martin. They looked shattered and seemed to have visibly aged, but they had succeeded in spite of the shortened rope, which was only just long enough for the job in hand. I was so pleased and proud. What a memorable special time we had, and although no new Munros were bagged, it didn't matter. As the man in the snow would say, 'A day in the mountains is never a waste'.

CHAPTER 10

Dogged Determination

June 2014

We were treated to easily accessible mountains at the end of 2013 then we had the drama of Skye in the first half of 2014, but the summer of 2014 was going to be rather different. It would come down to hard graft without the adrenaline boost of the Cuillin to help us on our way. In June we had a week at a cottage in Coulags, the same property we had stayed at while on our winter course. It was our third visit but it always felt special and evoked happy, if not some scary memories.

Maoile Lunndaidh kicked the week off. It was one of several where cycling in would have been hugely beneficial, but as it wasn't an option I never thought any more of it. I can't say what thoughts were going through Dave, Anita and Carl's minds as they had mastered the art of riding a bike. So no wheels and I felt poorly. The plumbing and stomach were being temperamental as usual. On every visit to Scotland I could nearly always guarantee one day in the week when I would have an issue. Pink medicine, paracetamol and ginger biscuits would normally do the trick and after two or three hours into a walk I would be fine. In those three hours I would remain silent, although I'm sure those around me appreciated the peace and quiet. Diane (remember, our sun-loving friend) once suggested I could opt out of a walk and couldn't understand, that was not an option. I still find that hard to explain.

It was a silent plod along the six mile track. Only two people passed us on bikes, as if we needed reminding. We eventually arrived at the start of the main approach to the mountain. The line of attack that Dave took onto Maoile Lunndaidh was relentless. I felt sure there was an easier angle we could have chosen, but I couldn't be bothered debating the issue so duly followed. Rather belatedly I got the bit between my teeth and resigned myself to being in for a long day with no shortcuts.

* * *

Another long haul was Lurg Mhor and Bidein a' Choire Sheasgaich starting from the Attadale Estate near Lochcarron where again a bicycle would have been useful. However, we were staying out overnight so two wheels were less important. After the enjoyable bivvy on the Cuillin Ridge the alfresco idea seemed appealing. Dave was keen and the weather was good enough. There was a bothy that could be utilised, but I had dismissed that idea as the weather was more than adequate to appreciate the outdoors and I was in good spirits. Probably the thought of another idyllic night bivvying on top of a mountain had some bearing. As we had to pass the bothy we paid it a brief visit; very nice but I didn't want a roof over my head. It was only then I sensed that Anita was paying particular attention to the interior design of Bendronaig bothy and realised not once had she spoken about bivvying.

The walk went well and we arrived on Cheesecake's summit. This is the nickname of Bidein a' Choire Sheasgaich, probably evolved over time by us Sassenachs south of the border, whose grasp of Gaelic is minimal at best. What a lovely summit, with a breeze blowing ensuring a midge-free zone. I was happily looking for a cosy spot to call my own when suddenly I became aware of Anita standing at my side and not looking overly happy. Carl was in diplomatic neutral mode. The summit was not for them. For some inexplicable reason hauling water uphill didn't appeal and therefore they proposed bivvying lower down near a lochan.

As I was a professional water bearer I wanted to remain on the summit and transporting water would be a small price to pay for another magical experience. Dave was in agreement and so the obvious solution was for everyone to do what they preferred. Carl was happy to accompany Anita and we would re-group as and when.

It was quite windy near the lochan and so it was Plan B for Anita and Carl as they headed for the bothy. We returned to the summit making a diversion to collect four litres of water. Dave offered to be the water carrier and I gracefully accepted. He was quite surprised just how heavy it was and of course I grabbed the opportunity to remind him that I had carried far more, and further, for his Cuillin traverse.

We had our meal of packet stew while admiring our surroundings. This was going to be such a romantic setting, or so I thought. However, the mountain had other ideas and before long the notorious clag descended. We still had a limited view but the inevitable happened and we could see nothing. We called it a day and snuggled down in our respective hidey holes. Staring up into clag wasn't quite what I'd envisaged so perhaps the twinkling stars were having the night off or shining down on some lucky person on the Cuillin Ridge.

* * *

We awoke to feel cold wet drizzle on our faces so an early start seemed the logical answer. It had been enjoyable to a certain degree but it proved that attempting to rekindle a magical moment from the past doesn't always work. The weather wasn't much better when we arrived at the bothy, but the kettle would be on and there would be a hot cup of coffee to enjoy. Except no, Anita and Carl were still asleep. Rattling the kettle and clattering the cups soon got them out of their sleeping bags. At least we could have a half-decent second breakfast with them, as our early bird version had consisted of a biscuit and black coffee. We wandered back to the car with everyone happy with the choices they had made.

July 2014

How long is long? What was regarded as a lengthy day at the start of the challenge became a normal day, but I suppose that was to be expected as the mind and body adapted to more severe regimes. However, I'm quite sure the Braeriach four will be remembered as a lengthy day for the foreseeable future. There was a chance to squeeze in a short stay in the Cairngorms so I booked three nights B&B in the Aviemore region. It was a wet July day and Anita, Dave and I were somewhat bedraggled as we had "popped up" a Munro (A'Mharconaich) en route from leaving North Yorkshire.

On arrival at our lodgings the welcome was a little cool. The door opened and the lady said hello, but at the same time her gaze was directed at our feet and she asked if we would mind removing our boots. We had removed our boots; they were clean trainers. The place was immaculate but perhaps not accustomed to hill-walkers. However, we did as she asked and once she accepted we were house trained, both she and her husband were charming and did whatever they could to help. I warned Dave to be careful where he placed items in the bedroom as everything was in varying shades of cream with beautiful broderie anglaise piping on the pillowcases and towels.

* * *

The following morning we drove to the Sugar Bowl car park below the Cairngorm Ski Centre. This was going to be a tough day in every sense of the meaning. Four Munros, involving a considerable amount of ascent, mileage and time. Braeriach, Cairn Toul, Sgor an Lochain Uaine and The Devil's Point. Three of the mountains are some of the highest Munros. Many people spread the route over two days, but we had read that the very fit could do it in one day. We were fairly fit and with the right attitude, anything would be possible. The determined approach was functioning well, and not even the midges were getting the better of me. Nor the fact that I was carrying possibly unnecessary weight in my rucksack in the shape of a pair of walking shoes. I had, and still have, an intermittent problem with my ankles when I cannot bear to have anything touching them, so boots can be a tortuous affair. Shoes seemed the only stopgap measure other than not walking, and that option was certainly not getting a look in.

Dave had warned me about the Chalamain Gap, a boulder-strewn ravine. However, on reaching this alleged obstacle it seemed quite acceptable on this dry sunny morning. I knew it was a notorious black spot for avalanches, but today it was a doddle. Dave commented that I may not enjoy this minor challenge quite so much when we had to return later that day. What a negative attitude.

There was excellent visibility until moments before we arrived on the summit of Braeriach and then the mist descended, perhaps conjured up by a magician as there had been no sign to indicate such weather. According to Mr Pugh, the mountains are comparable to women, with so many mood swings ... what does he mean?

Out of the mist came a solitary young man. We stopped and chatted for a while as of course a young man alone was quite acceptable. He enquired about our intended plans and Dave asked where he had come from. The answer was Poland. Without hesitation Dave replied, 'You must 'ave set off early, mate.' I felt sorry for the poor chap. Something had been lost in translation and the English sense of humour had fallen on stony ground as he looked totally blank. Dave clarified what he meant – where had he started his walk, and a normal conversation was resumed. We said our farewells and within minutes the mist evaporated as quickly as it had appeared, treating us to awe-inspiring views.

In front of us lay a huge expanse stretching as far as the eye could see, broken only by jaw-dropping corries hiding blue-green lochans. It may have been July but there were still patches of snow interspersed across the plateau and clinging to the rims of the crags. This was going to be a wonderful day.

It was Dave who found the never-ending boulders irksome when we were on Cairn Toul, but for some inexplicable reason I was mega positive, leaving Dave to trail on behind. The only slight niggle had been when to have breaks, with Anita happier to be more economical with rests in favour of an earlier finish. Unfortunately, this was not our style. For Dave and me to enjoy the day it meant having a break irrespective of the time and whether it was day or night. Anita was fine about the strategy and went along with our carry on. She was so accommodating and often commented how she appreciated having the opportunity to join us.

All four Munros had been bagged and I had enjoyed every one of them, but as we passed Corrour bothy my determined approach finally vanished into thin air. It seemed hours since our last rest and there had been no mention of a break, it was now 7.20pm and we were in the Lairig Ghru. This is a pass which cuts through the Cairngorm Mountains and the going underfoot leaves a lot to be desired. With weary legs the terrain became irritatingly annoying and I announced that at 7.30pm I would sit down no matter where I was and if that meant sitting in a bog, well so be it. Dave confessed he had become light-headed. So why did he leave it to ME to say something, knowing Anita wouldn't say anything?

Twenty minutes later after the luxury of a rest accompanied by food and drink we were happier bunnies and I dragged myself back into positive mode. That was until we reached the Chalamain Gap. It was nearly dark and begrudgingly I accepted that Dave was correct and the gap had totally lost its charm. Could we head higher and go right of the gap or possibly left of the gap? We couldn't agree and it was Anita who ended this "domestic". We had to choose the middle and go through the bloody gap. There were midges everywhere and the rocks I had merrily scrambled over many hours earlier had become loathsome ridiculous objects. The walking shoes I had trailed round with me all day hadn't been required and now I regarded the excess weight as a hindrance. (They would have been less than ideal but fell runners do not wear boots.)

At last we were on the final leg and although shattered, my concern was that we had another walk planned for the following day. To be more precise I was panic-stricken rather than merely concerned, but I needed to concentrate on the job in hand. Although the car was in close proximity there was a wood to walk through, it was pitch black and so I needed my head-torch. Could I hell as like find it! So amongst a rant and after the whole contents of my rucksack had been thrown into the heather, I found it in a side pocket, where I had allegedly looked minutes earlier. As I switched my head-torch on, Superman Dave, who seemed to have been born with night vision, just stood and smiled. You can imagine how well that went down.

Perhaps we didn't come into the category of "very fit" after all as it had taken us 16 hours and it was 11.45pm before we were reunited with Petal, our new car. My apologies, I should have introduced Petal earlier. She was Flossie's replacement. It had been a very sad day when we had to say goodbye to Flossie. I was close to tears as I handed her keys over, but she was getting a bit too old and so we had splashed out and bought a new Mondeo. With a little bit of imagination, her registration read Petal.

It was 1.00am before we got to bed. It would have been a little earlier but I couldn't switch the headlights off when we got back to the B&B. After a few minutes they went off but we had no idea how or why. Only when we spoke to the garage when we arrived home did they explain about these new-fangled lights which have a delay on, if you so wish. I must have caught a switch. I suppose that was the downside, or possibly a bonus, of owning an old car when you simply had them on or off.

* * *

The alarm was set for 6.00am. The proprietors couldn't believe our turnaround and that we'd missed having an evening meal. I couldn't believe it either. There was "only" one to climb, Beinn Mheadhoin, but it involved a considerable amount of ascent, descent and ascent before even reaching the mountain and then repeating it all again in reverse order to get back. It was one of many Munros with the adjective "inaccessible" or "remote" used to describe it.

We parked at the Cairngorm Ski Centre car park and dragged ourselves away from Petal. I have no idea how my body functioned for the first couple of hours, one foot in front of the other while bordering on throwing up. I have never taken drugs in my life, but at that moment had any illegal substance been offered to me which might have given me a boost I would have gladly taken it. We met two chaps on the lower slopes of Beinn Mheadhoin who were practising Tai Chi. At least I think that was what they were doing and it did cross my mind whether it would help my well-being. I would have tried ANYTHING.

After the first couple of hours I was functioning adequately, Anita was rather quiet and it was Dave who had become rather tetchy. The weather decided to add a little something to the day as the wind started to blow and then the rain began to fall. Oh dear, I'd forgotten I was in need of a new pair of waterproof trousers. Anita kindly gave me several safety pins to try and pull the gaps together.

The plateau of Beinn Mheadhoin has several tors or, in other words, big layers of rock on top of one another. The largest tor is the summit and it came as a shock to see how big this was with the rocks wet and slippery. Anita and I looked at one another in dismay. Now what were we going to do? Dave would manage, but would it be a case of socks over boots syndrome again? I could hardly believe my ears when Dave suggested we could forget about touching the top stone and miss the scramble out. What on earth had come over him? I retorted that we would do no such thing and if so, we would have to return another day. He agreed it was a lapse in attitude and with his help pulling and pushing Anita and me, we succeeded. Now it was a case of negotiating all the ups and downs again to get back to Petal. Nine hours after leaving her we were reunited, a mere stroll in the park.

CHAPTER 11

WILD WILDERNESS AND WILD WOMEN

October 2014

Going to Scotland for a week at a time had been a sensible change of strategy, but dabbling in two-week stints had its drawbacks. The first week worked well, but stamina, feet and legs struggled to cope with another week making the last couple of days of a two-week programme a toil of a pleasure. The first time we endured a fortnight we vowed it would also be the last. Of course, time healed the wounds and although two-week visits weren't the norm, they came in handy and solved the odd problem. Every cloud has a silver lining and the various high street chemists benefited with sales of painkillers, supports and foot-care products going through the roof. One day off per week had been factored in for seven-day stints but they were essential on two-week visits.

Perhaps we were being a little too optimistic in October 2014 with a two-week trip that included a wild camping trip. We spent a week near Loch Awe, to the east of Oban, along with Anita, Carl and friends, Lynne and Phil. Thirteen Munros were bagged including popping across to the Isle of Mull for Ben More via the A'Chioch ridge in glorious weather. The plan nearly went pear shaped as we only just managed to secure a booking on the car ferry. I never knew there was an annual car rally on the island, and if there had been enough time it would have been wonderful to watch it.

Lynne, Phil and Carl were due to head back home after the first week, but Anita, Dave and I were transferring to a favourite cottage further north in Kingussie ideally placed for access to a variety of mountain ranges. Carl and Anita knew we might have two nights wild camping immediately after leaving Loch Awe, subject to the weather. Carl could slightly extend his stay but had to be back at work on the Tuesday. This significant wild camping trip was to bag three Munros located in the north-west of Scotland, in a region known as the Great Wilderness and home to The Fisherfield Round. As the name implies, all the mountains are remote, with no easy or quick access even with a bike, but it's a spectacular, unspoilt area. Two further Munros are in the area, but Dave and I had climbed these before the challenge was born.

The Fisherfield Round actually comprises six mountains but one of the six has been demoted from Munro status. More accurate measurements thanks to technology had been the demise of poor Beinn a'Chlaidheimh, so strictly speaking it was unnecessary to call and see him, but I felt he should be visited.

When to visit the Great Wilderness was going to be a last minute decision for various reasons. Bridges are few and far in the Scottish mountains, and this route was no exception. Spring snowmelt could be an issue early in the year, or a prolonged spell of wet weather at any time of the year would mean that two unavoidable river crossings would be impassible. The midge season was a minor consideration and while Shenavall bothy was available, I had set my heart on wild camping for this trip. In any case, if we were visiting the area in the stalking season the bothy would be closed. And also, if it was the stalking season another issue would be ensuring that we weren't hindering the stalkers. It was hardly a doddle to choose a good time to visit.

Anita and Carl had been keen to partake in this particular trip, Anita in order to tick the Munros off and Carl because he loved wild camping. Unfortunately, the forecast for the weekend we left Loch Awe wasn't promising, but it looked excellent for the following week. Dave and I were in a quandary as this would mean Carl couldn't join us and yet the conditions were going to be perfect for camping. It required an objective opinion and Lynne was the provider. Without hesitation she said we should go camping and couldn't see why we were worrying. Carl wasn't actively Munro bagging, he didn't have a timescale to work to, it was our challenge and so what was stopping us? All of a sudden it was obvious we should grab the chance. We would go to Kingussie for a couple of nights then drive to Dundonnell for the wild camping and back again to Kingussie. Carl was fine about it and I expected Anita to be highly delighted, but I sensed some disappointment. For a while I couldn't fathom it out until the penny finally dropped. Dave and I wouldn't be climbing six mountains, just four and that would still be a big day. Anita knew we would happily return with her once our challenge was over and ensure that she got the other two bagged. However, had Carl accompanied us, Anita might have successfully persuaded him to branch off and include the other two Munros. This was the source of Anita's disappointment. I'm afraid I couldn't use the excuse that Anita had more stamina because she had youth on her side as I was 11 months younger.

So we packed our belongings from cottage number one, bagged another Munro before driving to Kingussie, then unpacked at cottage number two closely followed by filling the washing machine with dirty clothing. Thank heavens we were giving ourselves Sunday off.

* * *

With perfect weather conditions on the Monday we drove towards Dundonnell, grateful we'd taken full advantage of the conditions. Petal was left to her own devices at Corrie Hallie. It was a beautiful walk through some woodland as the burnished gold-brown leaves gently fell from the trees in the breeze. Shafts of mellow sunlight would reflect in the nearby burn, and we couldn't have wished for a more idyllic start.

We met some stalkers leaving for the day who were helpful and friendly, but then we had always found them so. The choice of route to take in autumn included checking various websites to enquire where stalking was planned, although it proved trickier for the estates that didn't partake in the system. But at least we tried.

The area we'd chosen to pitch the tent was the nearest we'd come to perfection. Flat, grassy and slightly concealed amidst several alder trees, with a river only feet away. It was sheer luxury to make camp in daylight and without battling against the elements. I took on my dutiful role as water bearer. It was a relief to see the Abhainn Loch an Nid was low as this was a river we would be crossing the following morning. We had the pleasure of a rather large fallen branch close at hand which acted as a comfortable bench and nicely accommodated the three of us. My blow up sleep-mat was just about fit for purpose. After the farce on the Seana Bhraigh trip Dave had repaired it, and although not 100% it remained sufficiently inflated for a good eight hours.

As the sun disappeared behind the mountains a flock of geese flew over squawking as they went. It's a sound I love but it seemed all the more special that particular evening. The stags could also be heard as this was the height of the rutting season – not exactly the same special feeling as the geese, but in keeping with our whereabouts.

Nobody suggested setting an alarm for an early start. I thought about it but kept my thoughts to myself as I felt sure we would wake early enough. Of course, Sod's law we didn't rise with the lark and it was near enough 9.00am before we left. Yes I know, too late, but we didn't have a train to catch, so would it really matter?

The first mountain would be the unnecessary mountain, Beinn a'Chlaidheimh, but first we had to cross our neighbouring river. I wore my crocs although the water was low enough to have left my boots on. However, as the crocs had been bought and packed especially for this purpose, there was a novelty factor to them so I had every intention of using them. Of course, that took extra time as once on the other side, they had to be exchanged for boots after having dried my feet with a flannel. Anita did exactly the same. I believe a comment was made implying that the paras or marines would be court martialled for such behaviour. Dave was doing the macho thing and kept his boots on. I suppose we were doomed already – a late start followed by sandals and flannels and we'd only gone a matter of yards.

Dave chose an acute angled approach on to Beinn a'Chlaidheimh, whose description of "fierce upper slopes" was accurate. Anita and I opted for a dogleg approach, which was a little further but less extreme. Even our route felt steep and, of course, I knew Dave would be doing his damnedest to beat us. Likewise, I was doing my level best to prove that female logic would win the day. I still say we won, although Dave contested that we were not at the agreed meeting point and he had won.

This was not dissimilar to the time we climbed Meall Glas and Sgiath Chuil near Crianlarich. I chose the steeper option due to a minor disagreement, the adrenaline had kicked in and I was going to show him. Dave had picked an easier gradient, and poor Anita, who was with us and not wishing to take sides, chose the middle ground. Yes, Dave got there first grinning away which made it all the more frustrating. I tried to disguise the fact that I was on the verge of collapse and Anita resembled a bloodhound with her tongue sticking out. I chose to sit separately and shared a grape with a bee that happened to come and sit with me. He was on my side, and more to the point he wasn't annoying me. Back to the Great Wilderness.

After making a slight diversion to the summit of Beinn a'Chlaidheimh I asked Dave why had we trailed up this one. I had totally forgotten it was me who had insisted on its inclusion, but Dave was quick to remind me.

The ascent onto the first Munro of the day, Sgurr Ban, was not pleasurable. It was a huge boulder-field, there was a cold wind blowing and most of the surrounding tops were covered in cloud. After endless encounters with rubble, we reached the summit and the first well-earned tick of the day was collected. The next stop and tick would be Mullach Coire Mhic Fhearchair. Although it was steeper than Sgurr Ban it had more character and was far more gratifying.

Anita was rather quiet, probably still wishing Carl could have been with us, but nevertheless she seemed quite happy. The extra stamina required to do the complete round would have been considerable and the enjoyment of the day could have been in jeopardy. Even if Dave and I hadn't already bagged the other two, I doubt our decision would have been any different. It seemed we had made good progress, but I easily forgot the distance to cover after the mountains themselves. We still had one more to climb, Beinn Tarsuinn, and as I glanced across at Meall Garbh I was extremely relieved that we could contour round that little obstruction to reach our goal. The final Munro of the day easily succumbed. Hooray, they were "done". But now the matter of returning to our tent.

Reaching the bealach was a nightmare and took far longer than anticipated. Dave noticed a ridge he reckoned we could have come down and it might have been easier, but it was too late to be changing tactics. We were losing daylight, but reached the faintest of trods (a tiny path) that followed the Abhainn Gleann na Muice down. This was to be our "handrail" as day turned into night. I didn't mind walking in the dark, but extra mental effort was required, it could be quite daunting and navigation had to be accurate. We were OK on that score, unless of course Dave keeled over. We still had two rivers to cross plus a notorious bog to negotiate, but I remained confident.

We eventually joined the path which came across from Carnmore. It was Dave who brought up the subject of distance, terrain and how long it could take. I sensed that he was tiring, which was quite understandable as he felt the responsibility was on him to return us safely. The map came out and Dave noted that a possible bothy appeared to be in the vicinity and perhaps we could stay there for the night. This was unexpected good news. I'd been on automatic pilot dutifully following, thinking that sooner, but probably later we would be reunited with the tent. Now there was a chance I could stop, and yes that sounded great so my engines proceeded to shut down. A thought occurred to me that the bothy could be locked as it was the stalking season, but I chose to dismiss this unsavoury possibility. A few moments later, I saw a couple of lights bobbing about, obviously some other people heading for the self-same place. I had mixed feelings about having to share, but tonight it would be acceptable. Except they weren't people at all, but a deer and his eyes reflecting in the beam of my head-torch.

We arrived at the building which had a rather nice veranda, but attractive porch or not, it was locked. I was a little disappointed, but the veranda would do. It could be a long night, but we would get some sleep and we had enough sandwiches to see us through. Dave had taken his rucksack off and I was about to sit down and get as comfortable as I could. But then I saw Anita, standing with her rucksack still on her back. I'd seen that pose on the summit of "Cheesecake". The idea of sleeping on the veranda wasn't well received. She was extremely polite but adamant that she wanted to continue and get back to the tent. Poor Dave was unsure which option to choose. Had it been open he would have opted to stay, but of course, that was not the case. For a few minutes there was an uneasy silence. Once my brain cells woke up from their premature slumbers I agreed that I would continue on the proviso that Dave would have the final say; negotiating rivers and a bog was a big ask of him. If he was in any doubt he must say and we would retreat to the veranda. Mr Pugh said yes.

It was only a couple of minutes before we arrived at the first river crossing. My crocs were in my rucksack and this river was one of the reasons I had taken them. But the novelty of swapping footwear had disappeared with the daylight. Both body and soul were still coming to terms with more being expected of them and suffice to say, I was a tad tetchy. The plus point was that the adrenaline had kicked in promoting a sudden burst of energy. I announced that I wouldn't be fiddling or faffing, certainly not looking for stones to stand on, and the sooner we accepted we would get wet the better. (Perhaps this was a premonition for 2015.)

With the head-torch on full beam, I glanced into the water and at the opposite bank; the water was slow moving and not very deep. I stepped off the riverbank into the ink-black water and in a purposeful manner waded across. Just this once I wouldn't be a humble follower and I would lead this section. I felt the cold water filling my boots, but didn't care. I had no idea if Dave and Anita were following, but I had no intention of stopping to see. The decision had been made and I was merely obeying orders. We all crossed, I calmed down and let Dave lead the way across the bog, followed by Anita and then me. Method in my madness – if I was the last I stood a better chance of avoiding the pitfalls of the bog. Women can be bitchy, and I have to confess I was half hoping Anita might lead the way through the bog.

Dave was doing his best to stay on a compass bearing but at the same time endeavouring to avoid the worst of the green slime-filled holes. And then he disappeared. He'd stumbled and fallen in a ditch. I was so worried I hardly dared to ask if he was injured. Mercifully, he was fine albeit a little muddy. Obviously, I was concerned for his welfare but had he been seriously hurt we would all have been in "deep doodah" in more ways than one. I managed to refrain from commenting that the veranda may have been a better choice. Oh, and before I go any further, in the unlikely event any experts are reading this story, please stop chuntering about the fact that we set off far too late for mid-October – I know that!

Dave did a marvellous job with his navigation and subsequently we arrived at the second river crossing. This was a more serious affair and the sound of rushing water could be heard some distance away. Fortunately, the moon was out lighting our way and illuminating the problem. This time nobody was tempted to leap in as the water was slightly deeper but running considerably faster. We couldn't afford to get this wrong so Dave was in charge. The three of us linked up and safely crossed together. Now we had an easy walk back and although it was late, or rather because it was late, I didn't see any point in rushing. A few minutes here or there was immaterial as we squelched with every step.

I decided to stop for a pee. Dave was with me and commented that there were now two moons out, positively stunning, but it was the one many miles away that took the prize for beauty. I looked skyward and there was another world, thousands of twinkling stars with shooting stars racing across the blue-black sky. The moon was our beacon with the odd wispy cloud floating by like gossamer wings. In an instant I forgot I was shattered, my feet weren't that cold and even my yearning for a hot cup of coffee had vanished into thin air.

Miracles do happen and we were reunited with the tent, but the idea of beans and sausage was dismissed. A sandwich and coffee would do. It was 11.30pm and I was tired, but I wasn't in any rush to retire to bed. Finally, I crawled into the tent and shuffled into my sleeping bag. Had it been warmer I would have happily slept outside, although the stags sounded rather too close for comfort. It was such a shame to be in a tent blocking the stars out. However, I wasn't to be disappointed as the silvery moonlight shone onto the leaves of the alder trees creating delicate silhouettes through the fabric of the tent. Sheer bliss save for the continual roar of the stags. Where are the stalkers when you need one? I jest!

Dave and Anita fell asleep but I was wide awake. With hindsight Anita had done me a favour because I was glad we hadn't stayed on that veranda. Funny how things work out. I decided some soothing music was required so the earplugs went in and my twinkly music was selected. The correct title is "Music from the Pleiades" by Gerald Jay Markoe. The Pleiades is a star cluster in the constellation of Taurus and the music was described as "suitable for relaxation, meditation and healing." The only items missing were perhaps candles and a few joss sticks burning here and there. I drifted into one of my special bubble worlds. I didn't want to sleep.

The silhouetted leaves had gone, it was light and I had slept like a baby. What a glorious autumnal morning. The river shimmered in the early sunshine – perhaps the fairies had polished it overnight – and the branches of the trees gently swayed in the breeze. There couldn't have been a better backdrop for our leisurely breakfast of much appreciated baked beans and sausage. We even had time on our hands, thank you, Anita.

Everything was packed away and we began the walk back to the car. The moon was still visible in the pink and blue sky. I begrudged leaving that beautiful rugged place so I walked a little way behind in order to walk on my own. I was in a fragile bubble and one that was about to burst, but for just a few minutes more I would do my utmost to cling to it.

CHAPTER 12

ODE TO OSSIAN AND ORCHY ORDEAL

February 2015

Storm force winds, high avalanche risk and whiteouts possibly lasting the week was the general gist of the mountain weather forecast. February 2015 was doing its best to upstage February 2014. The four of us were returning to North Ballachulish. Carl had managed to persuade his employers that they could manage without him for a week. Being in full-time employment he had to be selective about which trips he came on. However, if there was a chance of bad weather, Carl was more than eager to head north. Snow and sub-zero temperatures seemed far more alluring than hot sunny days. I have to say that Dave and I were in the same camp; it was Anita who was more suited to hotter climes.

As usual we had an itinerary, but before we even arrived at the cottage we knew this would drastically change. Whiteouts were one thing, but the risk of avalanches and storm force winds was a different ball game. Winds of 80 to 90 miles an hour meant our rest day would be taken on our planned Day One of Munro bagging. The forecast for the next day was considerably better, with only 40mph winds on the cards, but none of the nearby Munros seemed suitable to tackle because of the various avalanche warnings.

I had a notion to head towards Rannoch Moor and Loch Ossian. There are three Munros: Beinn na Lap, Sgor Gaibhre and Carn Dearg, all regarded as straightforward mountains. With an overnight stay at the youth hostel at Loch Ossian we could be successful in our mission. Some may find it incredible that this would be the first time I had ever stayed in a youth hostel. I had stayed in a couple of mountain huts/refuges in Slovenia, not through choice but out of necessity, and on both occasions we managed to book a private room. A private room or not, the standard of the toilets remained the same and could only be described as grim.

Although it was Sunday I had managed to contact the youth hostel direct, and a lovely lady by the name of Jan returned my call. She apologised for her absence when I first left a message, but she'd been busy clearing the snow from the platform at her nearby railway station, Corrour, a 20-minute walk away. She'd abandoned the idea due to the volume of snow and the speed it was covering her best attempts. Perhaps warning bells should have been ringing. However, excitement was deafening the tolling bells, so I made a booking for the four of us. We were in luck and could have one of the dormitories for our own personal use due to lack of demand. Yes, them there bells were well and truly clanging, but still I couldn't hear them.

We left the cottage at 6.45am and drove to Fort William to catch the early southbound train to Corrour. The train is the only form of motorised transport available as no public roads lead to Corrour. A charming thought which added to the appeal. The railway station is the highest mainline station in the UK at 1,339ft (408 metres) and this was the first time I'd seen a snowplough attached to the front of a train. We left a wet and miserable Fort William, but within a matter of minutes the scenery had been transformed into a snowscape. The railway crosses some of the most inhospitable areas of Scotland and would be a major engineering feat even in this day and age, but a near miracle and a tribute to the men back in the 1890s when it was built.

As the four of us stepped off the train we stepped back into our childhood, throwing snowballs and jumping in snowdrifts. Carl was all for making snow angels, until I pointed out that staying warm and dry for as long as possible would pay dividends. The boring adult head had returned. Had it not been for the Way Out signage, a compass may well have been needed to guide us off the platform. Huge snowflakes were falling accompanied by the wind. Balaclava and snow goggles were donned and 30 minutes later, 50% longer than it should have taken, we just about managed to make out the outline of the hostel. We were calling to leave our overnight gear, which included a bottle of red wine. Two bottles would have been better, but we were roughing it after all. You may have noticed that red wine has been mentioned on more than one occasion. As far as I'm aware, none of us had a drink problem and we only allowed ourselves a bottle of wine on the days when it had been particularly strenuous. It was not of our doing that the majority of Munros came under the self-same classification.

Jan greeted us in amongst sweeping the snow out of the porch. Another futile task because as soon as the door was opened the floor turned white at an alarming rate. We told her our plan of action, Carn Dearg and perhaps Sgor Gaibhre. She didn't seem unduly concerned but warned us that a father and son had been forced to turn back the previous day and gently reminded us that, 'People do die out there'. We assured her that we would turn back if required.

Off we went in close formation, Dave leading and breaking trail, with Carl bringing up the rear ensuring that Anita or I didn't disappear. We were no longer snow virgins and our previous experience was standing us in good stead as we tackled large snowdrifts and energy-sapping deep snow. Beneath us was a track, although at that moment it was a figment of the imagination. Conditions were about to get worse. The invisible track had the benefit of giving the snow a solid foundation, but now the snow concealed peat hags and watery hollows. At one stage Dave and Carl hauled me out of this white quicksand. One leg had disappeared into snow up to my thigh, with my foot still dangling in an empty space. We persevered a little longer and finally reached consolidated snow. We had gained the advantage of solid ground, but sadly the wind was increasing in strength, the snow was still falling and visibility was rapidly deteriorating. We'd reached a height of 2,600ft (800metres), but the difficult decision had to be made and it was agreed that we needed to turn back. Whiteouts are demanding in still conditions, but when you're also battling to stand up because of the wind and every item of clothing and gear is covered in a layer of ice, it feels more like a fight for survival.

We stopped for Dave to get his map out. He partially unzipped his jacket and in an instant the wind snatched his map case out of his pocket. I was the only one who saw it disappear as it happened so quickly. Initially, Dave didn't believe me, until of course he discovered an empty pocket. This was the first time I sensed fear but, thankfully, just for a fleeting moment. Carl's map was carefully removed from his rucksack and treated with the utmost respect.

As planned, we started to lose height only to realise we were off our correct bearing and needed to make an adjustment, which entailed a small amount of re-ascent. This wasn't ideal but for safety's sake it was the correct choice. Just before we altered course I shouted to Dave (due to the wind, not because I was annoyed) that I felt we were wrong. We returned to the invisible track to be greeted by snowdrifts that had grown in stature, but unfortunately the same couldn't be said for my little legs. I vaguely remember crawling over a drift as it was the easiest option. My goggles were frozen inside and out, along with my trekking poles that were covered in a fine layer of ice. Anita had inadvertently left her jacket pockets slightly open only to discover beautifully formed snowballs snuggled inside. Perhaps this is hard to believe unless you've experienced a blizzard.

It was a heartening sight to see the hostel once more. Four Eskimos shuffled into the porch and Jan met us with a welcoming smile, appearing pleased to see us back in one piece. We hadn't been the only head cases out that day. A lady of few words, perhaps in her early twenties, had also booked in. She'd been out on her own practising for some leadership qualification. I think she needed some practice in communication skills and a smile wouldn't have gone amiss, but hey ho. We saw very little of her as she spent most of the time in the other dorm.

There had also been another woman staying at the hostel but she'd left to catch the train having abandoned her plan of climbing Beinn na Lap. She'd fallen through the snow into a burn containing more than a smattering of water. It was interesting to note that there had been more females than men out that day. So to all intents and purpose we had the place to ourselves. It was perfect, in the middle of nowhere watching the snow falling, a roaring fire and a bottle of red wine. Another strenuous day.

One thought that crossed my mind was the location of the toilets, which were outside in a glorified shed. I always have to get up in the night no matter how little I drink. The prospect of getting togged up in full winter gear and venturing outside wasn't appealing. I shouldn't have worried as Jan was ahead of the game and placed a plastic potty in our dorm. Considering this was my first stay at a youth hostel and one that didn't have mod cons, I felt I was adapting remarkably well. I like my home comforts, but I was pleased that we didn't have modern facilities, which I'm led to believe most hostels now have. No fridge (well, that was hardly a problem), no washing machine, outside toilets and no shower seemed to be in keeping in such an environment.

* * *

The following morning we looked out to see blue skies, sunshine and very deep snow, but a fierce wind was still blowing. It looked a beautiful day, but there were ominous clouds in the distance so we decided to get the next train back. We might have managed Beinn na Lap, but the snow was so deep, and depending on what the weather decided to do it was by no means a certainty we would reach the summit. We hadn't bagged a single Munro, but I for one had enjoyed a most thrilling yet salutary 24 hours.

Not to be deterred by our zero tally at Ossian we proceeded to visit the Bridge of Orchy area on three consecutive days. The first visit was a success insofar as we bagged Beinn Dorain. Normally, this would be paired up with its neighbour, Beinn an Dothaidh. However, with our enthusiasm waning our progress was painfully slow due to the snow, poor visibility and windy conditions. Anita did everyone a favour when she announced that she was returning to the car and wouldn't be attempting the second Munro. She was tired, had stumbled on the way back down and was in some pain. We willingly returned with her, and deep down felt somewhat relieved.

* * *

The following morning we went back to the Bridge of Orchy minus Anita. Once more, the three of us trudged through the snow we had visited only hours earlier. This time it was easier going because of our old footprints and a substantial amount of snow had melted. We arrived at the bealach at the head of Coire an Dothaidh and did a hanger left, or to be a little more technical we headed in a northerly direction. There was a brisk wind blowing but we had good visibility and it wasn't snowing. Due to avalanche risks, Dave selected an indirect route, north and then east, that avoided cutting across possible unstable snowfields. So the west summit but not the main summit was our first target.

Dave was three or four hundred yards ahead of Carl and me. We were busy chatting, or perhaps it was just me nattering, but within a matter of minutes the gates of hell opened. The sky was black as night and I wondered what on earth Dave was doing as I saw him drop to his knees. I quickly realised that the wind had dramatically increased in intensity as it hit us like a train. Dave was more or less crawling to a rocky outcrop closely followed by Carl with me clinging onto him. We shuffled under the tiniest shelf of protruding rock, half sitting and half lying down. The strength of the wind was unbelievable, so we were not going anywhere. Carrying extra gear in winter is heavy and rather a pain in the neck when it isn't required, but this just proved, if proof were needed, the necessity.

So with an insulated jacket, waterproof jacket, balaclava, snow goggles, neck warmer and goodness knows what else, I was warm. After some 15 minutes the storm appeared to be abating. There was still a strong wind and we were in a whiteout but it was manageable. We aimed for the summit and after a couple of heart-stopping moments when I couldn't decipher left from right and was fully aware that the edge of the mountain wasn't far away, we safely reached our goal. We wasted no time in returning from whence we came.

We allowed ourselves the luxury of a break 100 yards above the bealach in the shelter of a rock face. Although every item of clothing and equipment was covered in frozen snow I was warm and dry. Unlike down, the advantage of a synthetic insulated jacket is that it's less important if it gets wet and it can be worn over the top of anything. This avoids the chilly and awkward manoeuvre (particularly in bad weather) of taking a jacket off in order to add an additional layer underneath before replacing the jacket. Dave had used this "over" technique for years and I would say how silly it looked. Of course he was right – who cares about looks in bad weather? (One size larger than normal is required for this to work.)

Our break over and I resembled Nanook of the North, but I was happy and looking forward to an easy walk back down the corrie. I was wrong. The bealach had become Nature's version of a spin-dryer. With the wind being funnelled it had formed a vortex. I could just about stand but couldn't move. Dave went in front facing towards me and Carl went behind, which worked quite well. Dave is a good 6 feet tall, Carl is perhaps 5 feet 10 and sturdy, and I was the sandwich filling. For just 50ft or so it was like a "push me pull you" as I was manhandled down that section. I can assure you the push me pull you sandwich was about as erotic as Dave in the tent with Anita smelling of Deet with a midge net over her head! It didn't take long to drop out of this maelstrom and to our surprise we met four other souls out in this weather. It appeared that one might have been a mountain guide. They commented how lively the weather had been, but everyone was smiling. The remainder of the day was rather uneventful and by the time we arrived back at the car boring normality had resumed.

Our final tally for the week was two. You are correct in thinking I mentioned three visits. We also started a walk north of Bridge of Orchy at Achallader but again failed to reach a summit. Our speciality had been trudging through deep snow, reaching heights of over 2,600ft (800 metres) only to be beaten back by high winds. Anita joined us on our last attempt, but the strong wind wasn't doing her bruised back any favours and there was a limit to how many painkillers could be taken per mountain. We resigned ourselves to Nature having the last word.

April 2015

Two months later and we were back on the Ossian trail. We were based further east in our Kingussie cottage. We drove to Tulloch railway station to catch the train to Corrour. Wall to wall sunshine greeted us and rather than adding layers of clothing, it was a case of casting off and regretting I hadn't worn shorts.

We called to see Jan at the youth hostel bearing gifts of milk, wine and tobacco for her rollups. She was expecting us as I'd been in touch asking if it would be OK for us to use the facilities prior to catching the last train back. With excellent weather we hoped to bag all three Munros in one day starting with Beinn na Lap, followed by Sgor Gaibhre and then Carn Dearg. Jan was pleased to see us – or perhaps it was because we had her tobacco. Living in a remote location meant a train journey to the likes of Fort William for an extra pint of milk or tobacco. Contractors and diggers were in the area working on improvements to various utilities but there had even been talk of possible modernisation of the hostel. That would be such a shame.

I was on top form with very much the determined approach, but poor Anita was having foot trouble caused by a pair of new boots. In order to allow some comfort she was swapping trainers with boots and vice versa. So whatever wasn't being worn had to be carried in her rucksack.

I thoroughly enjoyed Beinn na Lap which was an easy mountain in such conditions, but also a lovely Munro that had character. I even saw a beautiful lizard as I plodded up the hillside, happy in my own little world. Occasionally, I would look back towards Loch Ossian and watch tiny ripples just breaking the surface. In the distance were the other two Munros of the day – what a difference from our February foray, but not necessarily better.

Dave had devised a route that would take us to the start of our second Munro. It would be slow going underfoot and some bog hopping would be required, but our immediate obstacles were in the form of fairly steep snowbanks. Some were avoidable while others could be carefully negotiated, once Anita had changed into the appropriate footwear.

To the north of Corrour shooting lodge, we headed for an intermediate top that ultimately would take us to Sgor Gaibhre. Dave suggested I might like to lead the way as the determined approach was shining brightly. I had read about an easy angled approach but as I puffed and panted, at the same time getting far too warm, I came to the conclusion that this was not what I would call easy. Needs must so I carried on, and not until I reached a plateau did Dave point out that I'd taken the direct approach. Of course, he wasn't going to stop me, Mr Pugh being a lover of "direct". There were several snowfields to cross before arriving at the third Munro of Carn Dearg. However, they had aided our progress in areas that would normally have been boggy. We made our way off the summit and reached the section we'd attempted back in February. The minefield of peat hags and bogs, now fully exposed, justified some of our tribulations in winter.

We arrived back at the hostel thrilled with our achievement. Unlike our February visit, several people were staying and we chatted, in amongst eating our mandatory beans, sausage, toast and red wine. I decided to sit outside by the loch as it was too warm inside and it seemed a waste to be cooped up within four walls. It was a stunning evening. The sun was slowly setting casting reflections across the water. Beinn na Lap was immodest showing himself in all his glory, yet another equally special moment at Ossian.

Reluctantly, we started the walk back to the railway station to catch the last train. I may have been reluctant to leave, but my wish to stay a little longer could have become a reality. The train arrived, and as usual after spending another magical time in the mountains I chose to stand on my own a little way down the platform. That was until I realised the door on the train was locked. Luckily, the guard on the train ushered me to the open door. Dave was totally oblivious that I wasn't on the train. Of course my dear husband pointed out that it was my fault.

Many years ago I was left behind in the Lake District when we were catching a coach. Dave thought I was on the coach but didn't check. There were six others who also missed the coach so we headed for the nearest pub and a couple of drinks later I found it quite amusing. Dave and I were reunited a few hours later and luckily for him I still saw the funny side.

CHAPTER 13

BALMY OR BARMY LINN OF DEE

May 2015

Our long days in 2014 had proved good grounding for 2015. But ignorance is bliss. I had booked several weeks close together over April and May when cottages were cheaper to rent and with the added bonus of a goodly amount of daylight hours. If we were lucky we could possibly have some half-decent weather. To think we once vowed not to dovetail weeks together. This was our last year and I felt we had grown in strength in a variety of ways.

We were back in our Glenshee cottage. It was lovely returning to certain properties. Three in particular fell into this category where they felt like home from home, where we knew what to expect and vaguely remembered how the various appliances worked. Dave detested state of the art hobs that required a degree in engineering to fathom out how to switch the damned things on. 'What's wrong with old-fashioned knobs?' he would chunter as he pushed and prodded various symbols – well, there wasn't a lot I could say to that statement.

Glenshee wasn't the ideal place to be based as the Munros on the agenda were further north in the Linn of Dee. I hadn't been able to find a cottage close to the area that took my fancy. There would only be one loo, or the decor looked a bit dubious, there would be no dishwasher (well that was a definite no) or if it looked promising it was already booked. Anyway, as I would be doing the driving, a 40–50-minute journey each way didn't seem that much of an issue in the great scheme of things. So as usual I decided on which mountains we could do along with choosing where we stayed and then ran it by Dave. By 2015 I had become considerably more proactive in the route finding business, sometimes to Dave's dismay. Gone were the days when I dutifully followed, not questioning his decisions.

Three days prior to leaving for Glenshee an old foot problem of Dave's reared its ugly head. He'd been given a cortisone injection in his toe 18 months earlier, but now, of all times, it had stopped working. Within a matter of hours Dave had gone from walking normally to struggling to put one foot in front of the other. My heart sank when I saw him hobbling along. I was sorry he was in pain, but anxious that the proposed Munros could be in jeopardy. Unfortunately, just about all the routes planned were lengthy and arduous even by Munro standards.

We were in company when without thinking, I snapped at Dave telling him he would just have to take as many painkillers as necessary. Our friends looked at me in total disbelief at the well-hidden compassion for Dave. I felt quite ashamed. Diane reiterated what she'd said at the outset of the challenge. The deadline was not set in stone and the world would not end if I exceeded the time limit. Of course, she was right, but in my mind it was vitally important that my goal was achieved by the original rules of play. There was no time to see the consultant before our departure to Scotland, but we remembered how he had strapped Dave's toe as a temporary measure. Perhaps our adventures were beginning to take their toll on our less than youthful bodies.

I was also having problems with my ankle. I'd been to see a podiatrist who had prescribed orthotic insoles and rest. She must have read my mind when rest was mentioned. It was literally a case of "talk to the hand as the feet are not listening". She went to great lengths to point out that if I ignored her advice a ligament might snap and then I wouldn't be walking anywhere. I opted to take heed of the insole advice but rest would come when I was back at work. The trip to the Linn of Dee began with some trepidation.

The date was 10th May and it was debatable whether or not we should carry winter gear. Although there was snow about it appeared rather patchy so we decided against it. Carn a'Mhaim and Derry Cairngorm in the Cairngorms were on the agenda so it came as no surprise when the cloud enveloped the tops. When in doubt, head for the cloud and you'll probably find a Munro hiding somewhere.

It had been an easy passage reaching the summit of Carn a'Mhaim, but the mountains had decided it was time to remind us who was boss, and it certainly was not us. We were aiming in the direction of Ben Macdui before heading to a bealach at 4,098ft (1,249 metres) – higher than many Munros. This required negotiating a boulder-field. I wasn't a lover of them at the best of times and to add to the enjoyment, snow was lurking on and between the rocks. Some of the snow was soft, some compacted, some deep and some a mere smattering. Just for good measure the visibility had deteriorated dramatically and a rather strong wind was now blowing. It felt rather like Russian roulette deciding which boulder to perch on, only to be thrown off balance by a gust of wind into a snow-filled crack. Then it was at the toss of a coin whether your foot disappeared down a mini crevasse or, if luck was on your side, the snow would hold your weight. This palaver went on for quite some time with the wind growing in intensity.

Tiny ice pellets were now peppering our faces, and the goggles came out along with the map. We could see sweet Fanny Adams. Dave hesitated for quite a while and I could see concern in his face, but I daren't ask if his foot was hurting. He quickly regained his usual confident aura and we went a little further. By the time we reached the approach onto Derry Cairngorm it had become a real battle to advance. We reached the summit not quite on hands and knees, but an upright position couldn't be assumed. Leaving the summit was just as tricky and yet I was revelling in getting a real battering from the wind. Looking back I strongly believe that I operated far better in adverse conditions.

As we lost height we came out of the madness and into benign conditions. Dave's foot was fine but I was hobbling as the sore ankle issue had returned and a blister had developed between my toes. This was the first time in years I'd suffered with a blister. Day One of a two-week stint, with 12 hours of walking, 20 miles and a good 7,000ft of ascent, meant two Munros were in the bag but the feet weren't fit for purpose. Perhaps this was my comeuppance for my uncaring attitude towards Dave with his issues.

* * *

The following day was a much easier affair with Beinn Bhreac and Beinn a'Chaorainn, and we were out less than 10 hours so barely worth a mention. The old man's feet were satisfactory, but rather than taking only one day off in the week, Dave thought a second day of rest would help. This was a good idea, but how could we still accommodate everything on our agenda? Dave solved the problem when he suggested that we combine Ben a' Bhuird with Ben Avon. A day would be gained but at the cost of a huge day by putting these two together. He thought his feet would still benefit even though they would be in for a real pounding when we bagged the duo.

Ben a' Bhuird and Ben Avon are big boys in height and both are home to enormous plateaux in the Cairngorms. Severe weather trundling across these high expanses would be a very serious and sobering thought. However, unless the weather forecasters were totally wrong, we shouldn't have any worries on that score.

We drove past the Linn of Dee on the way to the Linn of Quoich armed with our crocs ready for the big day. There was a strong possibility that crossing the Allt an Dubh Ghlinne would require wading due to the amount of snowmelt. I gambled on leaving my boots behind and wore my walking shoes (aka approach shoes) as anything touching my ankle had become so painful. Water would be a major feature that day, but it was rather a surprise when there was an enforced diversion into the trees from the main track. A huge swathe had been washed away, presumably months earlier when Scotland had been hammered by storms. The crocs were needed on reaching the burn and even Dave agreed to use them. You would be correct in thinking this would be a simple procedure – removing shoes and socks, wade, dry the feet off and back on with the footwear. Fine if the feet weren't adorned with a variety of extras:

Piece of sponge between the toes

Compeed (other makes are available) on the blister

Plaster on the little toe

Gel ankle support protecting a layer of anti-inflammatory cream

Oh and just for good measure a knee support, but by rolling that up it could stay put.

Keeping the various items dry or replacing them was laborious and time-consuming. All three of us had similar issues. Dave had his toe strapped up and Anita had foam, plasters and an ankle bandage to care for thanks to her new boots. Had we been on one of Martin's courses, I felt sure such behaviour wouldn't have been tolerated. Other than the 30 minutes we wasted with the foot procedure we were making good progress, I was in good spirits and we reached the summit of Beinn a'Bhuird without further ado.

It had been mooted that we could wait until Ben Avon summit to have a proper break, but as we had already stopped I grabbed the chance to have a bite to eat. Ben Avon seemed too far away for my liking. Everything was going well until we approached the bealach, The Sneck. No doubt in normal circumstances the descent into The Sneck would hardly be noticeable, but there was a slight technical hitch barring our way in the shape of one enormous snowbank. We weren't carrying ice axes or crampons and, of course, I had no boots ... bugger. I saw a possible diversion but Dave described my suggestion as a day's walk in itself, not a diversion. He had other ideas as he tested the snow and although reasonably firm it wasn't rock hard. Dave went first kicking steps in as I gingerly followed with trekking poles to steady myself. He had done the hard work making it comparatively easy to follow. Next stop Ben Avon.

I was going great guns, striding out and feeling a little smug, with Anita and Dave some distance behind. Refuelling on Beinn a'Bhuird had paid dividends so I was going to make the most of this brief moment. We re-grouped on Ben Avon and scrambled up the tor onto the summit where we met a couple. They'd been watching us descend the snowbank and were taken aback when they asked what our planned route was. It made a refreshing change to meet people who were going at an even steadier pace than us.

It was a lovely sunny afternoon as we came off Ben Avon and followed the Glas alt Mor. Yes, more sunshine. Perhaps I've mentioned sunshine, snow and gales quite often. There were many times when it was purely wet and miserable, but as we didn't see anything and because there were no incidents along the way, those mountains haven't been included. No doubt an experienced writer could eloquently describe several unremarkable mediocre days, but as you will have gathered, I don't fall into that category.

There was a considerable amount of soft snow choking the gully alongside the stream and snow-bridges had formed that had seen better days. There was a time when we wondered who should test the stability of a particular snow-bridge. It was in the perfect place to aid our progress and yet the strength of it was debatable and we could see the cold and fast flowing water below. We discussed the physics or maths behind the conundrum. Do you send the lightest person first or the heaviest? By the same token, do you use the same footsteps or make new ones some distance away? Extra use may weaken the footsteps and so on and so on.

After nearly 50 years those absurd problems given to me in my maths lessons may have in actual fact proved useful. You know the type I mean: if Fred sets off at 8.00am carrying two bags of apples and John sets off at 7.30am carrying three bags of apples but he has a bike … snore, snore. Wake me up when that bright spark waving frantically at the teacher answers correctly. I think it goes without saying that our test pilot of snow-bridges was Mr Pugh in the absence of Carl.

Today we didn't have any test drives for Dave and although it was going to be a long day everyone was enjoying themselves on this glorious balmy afternoon. My approach shoes were serving me well. There was even hilarity when on stopping for a breather Anita's rucksack toppled over into a burn and started floating downstream. Admittedly, Dave and I found it more amusing than Anita, although she did have a chuckle. That was until she discovered her GPS, which was attached to the outside of her rucksack, had ceased to function along with her smartphone. Had it been my bog basic £19.99 pay-as-you-go phone the damage would have been less painful. (You'll be pleased to know some days later, both gizmos came back to life.)

We were a good 10 hours into the walk and aiming for a path which ultimately would reach a track. This so-called path hadn't seen life form pass its way in years. If we had disturbed the wild man of Borneo I wouldn't have been surprised, and a machete would have been handy as the terrain went from bad to worse.

Someone had flicked a switch as I suffered a serious sense of humour failure. I could see a decent path, but there was a river between us and it. After some nagging and heated exchanges, Dave agreed that if I wanted to cross the Quoich Water that is what we would do. It wasn't too deep and we did have the crocs. Dave went first, but he didn't wait. I'd rattled his cage and had asked just one too many questions. I noted that he took an indirect dogleg approach to the other side. It was fair to say I was a little disgruntled, so as a matter of principle I would select my own more direct route. I was two-thirds of the way across and all was well with the water just above my knees, but I liked the look of some very calm water just ahead of me. I now understand the saying "still waters run deep". The water was calm but deep. I hesitated, but the only thought that ran through my mind was, 'I'm going to get wet'. What a bizarre thought when I wasn't a natural in water. I learned to swim at school in spite of, or because of, the swimming teacher pushing me away from the sanctuary of the pool-side with a bloody long pole. It was most certainly a case of sink or swim, and fortunately the latter was the outcome. Thank heavens Dave had been observing me and read my crazy mind. He bawled at me to stop, and I obeyed. Perhaps it was hysteria as I lashed out with my trekking poles furiously threshing the water, directing verbal abuse at the river but feeling totally trapped. Dave managed to persuade me to divert to his route. Anita arrived a few moments later rather bewildered by the events but kept a safe distance while Dave and I had words. He was probably correct in reprimanding me, but it did little to quell the nerves. I offered to throw myself back in the river if Dave so wished, but mercifully he remained silent.

I calmed down but was a little subdued and walked some distance behind staring into the river. We arrived at yet another crossing involving water, but this time I did exactly as I was told. My confidence had been swept away downstream. This wading novelty had worn thin as we arrived at yet another crossing, the one that had been our first water crossing of the day. We arrived back at Petal 13 hours after we had left her, a great relief with not a stream or river in sight.

It was an hour's drive back to the cottage when the petrol warning light came on. I was sure we'd be OK, but when Dave suggested I should drive economically, I conformed and did my best. Eating at unearthly hours had become acceptable and was now part of the package. Sitting down to our evening meal at 11pm with the odd glass or two of red wine felt fine. The watery traumas were forgotten and we raised our glasses to a great balmy, or had it been a barmy, day?

* * *

Petal had been up and down the A93 more times than I care to remember and by now she knew where to find the car park at Linn of Dee. Today was going to be another long haul, with Carn an Fhidhleir and An Sgarsoch. Both were described as remote and infrequently visited, where the aid of a bicycle was strongly recommended. We knew we would certainly equal our 13-hour Ben Avon day, if not exceed it, without the use of pedal power.

The day started with the advantage of a good track for the long walk in to reach the mountains and yes, it was another sunny morning. Much to our surprise we met several people heading towards us and discovered they were on the TGO challenge. This is an annual event organised by *TGO* magazine that involves walking across the Highlands from west to east. We felt so sorry for one man who was in a dreadful state, with his legs visibly wobbling as he staggered about the track. He intended to abandon the challenge once he reached Braemar. Had he been happy to wait several hours at the car park for our return, we would have willingly given him a lift.

There were more water crossings to contend with, but only one warranted the crocs and a pair of Marigold rubber gloves. I thought I'd come up with a brainwave to wear rubber gloves on my feet with rubber bands around my ankles, the idea being that the gloves would keep the various wound dressings dry. You may mock, but my feet were warm in the cold water, although I confess they didn't stay dry. Back to the drawing board – I'm sure most inventors have teething problems.

We met three chaps who had cycled in and were heading for the same mountains as us. We took a slightly different approach to them that resulted in a 200 yard advantage for us. It wasn't intentional, but an imaginary race had developed. What do you expect when you've been walking for four hours before even reaching a mountain without a blizzard or howling gale to occupy your mind? Initially, Dave's pace subtly increased and Dave isn't renowned for being subtle. I barely noticed until he upped the ante once more and then the penny dropped. I too joined in which was most unlike me, unless, of course, they'd been fit females wearing figure hugging lycra.

The sunny morning had been replaced by cloud and drizzle that was turning to rain. We really needed to stop to put our waterproof trousers on but that would mean critical seconds lost in the "pit lane", so we carried on. Anita was a little way behind and I sensed that she wanted to dress for the weather. I kept thinking we would reach the summit but each hillock we went over proved we weren't quite there. We were getting wet so I allowed myself one more minute of this race and then I would quit. Thankfully, the summit appeared and the chequered flag came out. Waterproof trousers also came out of hiding, but Anita wasn't best pleased. Dave did politely say that any one of us was free to stop at any time. A few minutes later and the three men arrived on the summit. I doubt for one moment they were aware of the make-believe Formula One race which had just taken place.

We went on to the second Munro, An Sgarsoch, in mist, wind and rain, but we'd bagged the last Munro in the area. We met up with our three friends, all cheerful souls, and laughed about the inclement conditions. They commented about the two women, one man combination and felt that Dave was a lucky man. Dave laughed, 'You think so … if only you knew.' To us we were just three people bagging Munros. However, they weren't the first ones to comment on the male/female ratio. Back in 2013 we met one very well spoken gentleman on Beinn A'Ghlo, acknowledging his 200th Munro. He genuinely seemed a little envious of Dave, so rather than shatter his dreams Dave let him think whatever he wanted to think.

On dropping down to a well-made path the weather improved. The men on their bikes had long since gone and all that was left for us was the walk back to the car. It had been 14 hours and the Linn of Dee was done, but it had nearly "done" us.

The Chalamain Gap- Take One.

View from the tent in the Great Wilderness.

Early morning sky in the Great Wilderness.

Dave outside Loch Ossian February 2015.

Loch Ossian Youth Hostel in the distance.

Heading for the safety of the Youth Hostel having aborted the plan of action.

April 2015 Loch Ossian. Two months later on a beautiful spring day.

Relaxed, only minutes before the "spin-dryer" experience.

Wading before the novelty wore off.

Safely down but we should have taken crampons.

The pinnacles after Sron Coire Dhomhnuill.

The summit of Carn Eige in full winter conditions, 18th May.

The idyllic secluded beach.

The Team.

The Grey Corries.

Sunset at the end of a magical day in The Grey Corries.

31st December 2015-Fionn Bheinn Summit.

Friends Past and Present.

Fionn Bheinn left in peace.

The Happy Couple.

CHAPTER 14

AGONY AND ECSTASY IN AFFRIC

May 2015

It had been a successful week in the Linn of Dee, but we left the cottage on a muted high. Dave's feet were holding up, although we still had another week ahead of us with more epic routes to contend with. We packed our bags and moved further north and west to visit Glen Affric, an area known for its outstanding scenery. Carl had persuaded his boss to sanction unpaid leave and met us at our base in Drumnadrochit. There were two routes in particular that were meaty in their own right but on approaching our new base the neighbouring mountains were covered in snow. A beautiful sight, but this was going to make the mountains a far more serious proposition, and was something we could have done without.

We allowed a warm-up day of hopefully no more than eight hours duration in readiness for the arduous routes. However, pondering on what we could manage without wasn't the right attitude. Crampons were left behind, but luckily ice axes were taken. With hardly any snow on the ridge on to Toll Creagach we thought we'd been clever, but as we headed off in the direction of Tom a'Choinich we came to an abrupt halt. There was a lot of reasonably firm snow and although the ice axes saved our bacon, it was a bad judgement for the first day in the mountains.

Not January, not February, but on 18th May full winter gear was packed. The crocs were abandoned and so were the walking shoes, although that had been one correct decision I had made the previous day. We had three Munros to climb: Carn Eige, Beinn Fhionnlaidh and Mam Sodhail, which were all connected by ridges making a fine horseshoe. With Beinn Fhionnlaidh way out on a limb that would mean a time-consuming detour. Even in perfect conditions the route came under that charming category "epic" so with the snow it could be "mega epic".

Dave set off at a ridiculously fast pace and even Carl commented on it. Once I finally caught up to speak with Dave, I strongly suggested that he slowed the pace down both for my well-being and also if he knew what was good for him. This early hitch in the proceedings had a negative effect on my attitude and I feared that the challenge was becoming tarnished and routine.

Just for a change we reached a river that required crossing, but my mood was turning blacker by the minute as of course my crocs had been kicked out of my rucksack. We seemed to trail about backwards and forwards looking for the best spot to cross. What one person thought was OK another was not so sure about. The little patience I had was wearing thin, "we" were being too fussy, and although I had no intention of making the foolhardy mistake of heading for deep water, I felt that the sooner everyone accepted we wouldn't be bone dry after the crossing then so much the better. I chose to take my socks off, remove the insoles from my boots and just wear the boots. The riverbed appeared too slippery and sharp to go barefoot. I crossed successfully, albeit my boots filled with water, but considering the depth of the water that was to be expected. Carl crossed by some amazing balancing act on rocks, while Dave and Anita faffed about trying to stay dry. However, this gave me time to empty my boots, replace the insoles and put my socks on followed by plastic sandwich bags over each sock. My negative outlook had been superseded by a tetchy but determined approach.

The route to the first Munro, Carn Eige, was not only lengthy in time and effort but consisted of additional mountains and ridges and although they didn't hold Munro status, it was challenging and held potential hazards. Just below Garbh bealach we were met by deep snow everywhere and sunglasses were needed due to the brightness of the white blanket with the warm sunshine beaming down. Three of us thought it felt warm, but Anita concluded that it was less cold. Dave made the footsteps and I followed on with my mood noticeably changing for the better, and although Carn Eige was still some way off, at last the sparkle had returned.

We reached the base of Sron Garbh, which looked rather more serious and technical with all the snow cosseting it. It was rather like a mini Forcan Ridge so ice axes and crampons came out and the winter skills were about to be put to the test. Normal positions were assumed with Dave leading and Carl bringing up the rear. The adrenaline was pumping, but this was exciting. There were a couple of manoeuvres that warranted serious contemplation and I was reminded to trust my equipment. I took a leap of faith and with much relief I stuck fast to the mountain. Easier than the Forcan Ridge, but without the reassurance of a rope there was little room for error. My less than dry feet had become a distant memory as more important issues were now occupying the old grey matter.

A fairly slender arête was the next obstacle. I'm quite sure that minus the white stuff it would have been straightforward, but the snow emphasised its slender form – or was it just a trick of the light? It was at this point that Anita suggested we went back. My mouth dropped open, but I never uttered a word. Dave and Carl assured Anita that she would be fine and we would work as a team. The bottom line was that we were not going back. I was relieved, and my determined approach was now in overdrive. To have come this far and then retreat didn't bear thinking about.

We edged along the ridge until we arrived at some pinnacles. These were large jagged pointy lumps of rock that can be bypassed with the use of a side path. The pinnacles came as a surprise to Dave even though I had told him about them and shown him a photograph. But of course he hadn't paid attention. There were two reasons for this behaviour: 1) He was still coming to terms with my proactive involvement in route finding, and 2) He believed in using a map and referring to the SMC Munro book. Generally speaking, any other source of information rarely got a look in, his philosophy being, 'Years ago they had to fathom it out themselves and if you need a step-by-step guide you shouldn't be in the mountains'. Yes, I agree, quite an arrogant opinion, but I know what he meant in an age when people venture into the hills and mountains with nothing more than a smartphone with an app or the like.

Sadly, this particular day the bypass path didn't exist as it was buried beneath the snow. Oh dear, what a pity, or similar words went through my mind. Pick and mix was the plan of attack consisting of mild scrambling and some contouring round with the men in close proximity. Crampons were on and off dependent on whether the section we were on was bare rock or otherwise. Crampons feel great on snow and ice but using them on exposed rock seems more hazardous to me. To those into mixed climbing, I take my hat off to you. I might add that it wasn't just me who was on and off with the crampons.

At last, the comforting reassurance as we reached easy terrain with only soft snow as a hindrance and not a footprint to be seen. We arrived at the summit of Carn Eige with views as far west as Skye and east towards the Moray Firth, amazing and a real reward. It had "only" taken seven hours to reach the first Munro with just another two to go. There was a brief discussion whether to stick with our original plan and include Beinn Fhionnlaidh. It would make for a truly lengthy day particularly with the winter conditions, but if we omitted it an additional visit would be needed at a later date. It was verging on a unanimous decision to go for it. Nobody said no and silence was taken as a yes vote. Providing we were safe it made sense to carry on and if it took until midnight then so be it.

Heading down to Bealach Beag required great care. There was less snow but it was wet and slippery. My enthusiasm started to wane as Beinn Fhionnlaidh seemed further away as we walked towards it. Was he shuffling away when our backs were turned? Whether he shuffled or not, he was bagged and it was the first time the sun had disappeared. I looked westward to see menacing black clouds gathering. They had an uncanny resemblance to the storm clouds on our "spin dryer" day. If they came much closer we could be seeking shelter pretty darn fast. We opted not to say anything to Anita as she wasn't having the best of days. The clouds got nearer but appeared to be so heavy they were struggling to get over the various mountain ranges between us and them. It started snowing, the cloud base lowered and it was a little breezy, but that was as bad as it got.

Heading back uphill, more or less from where we had come, pushed the willpower to its limit. Anita was more positive in her outlook while I chuntered and complained about boulders and rocks moving beneath my feet. However, once we reached the base of Mam Sodhail the positive head returned and at last number three was within spitting distance. Neither Dave nor Carl seemed to have different mood variations, they just had an on/off setting. But I suppose men aren't as finely tuned as the female species.

It was early evening, the temperature was dropping and the snow was feeling firm. I was the first to decide that crampons were going back on irrespective of what the others may choose. Over the past three years I had noted, particularly with the men, a reluctance to be the first to succumb to crampons. Once one had made the decision the others happily followed. I think it was some macho, testosterone-based decision. I needed all the help I could get to remain upright, so if it meant putting crampons on in a car park, that was fine by me. Dave quickly followed suit, as the higher we got the icier it became. 7.45pm and the summit was reached – hooray!

There was a fair amount of daylight hours left and it was easy to forget it was mid-May with the snowscape more akin to mid-winter. We had a break but Dave was a little quiet, which I knew from past experience was not a good sign. He announced that he was going to check our intended way off the mountain. I was busy eating my corned beef and beetroot sandwich, trying desperately hard not to get the beetroot juice down my jacket but failing miserably. Mr Leader Man returned. It was as he suspected, totally blocked by a huge cornice and the headwall was choked in snow. After pulling Carl to one side, followed by some whispering and furtive looks, the men announced a revised route. For those who may be interested, it was down the ridge towards Mullach Cadha Rainich and then off that ridge into Coire Leachavie. I chose not to ask any questions until we were safely below the snowline. Then I was very polite and asked if this had always been the planned escape route. You know, the route that should always be in your "back pocket". Dave and Carl nodded a tad sheepishly with the word 'Yes' somewhat mumbled. I left it at that and accepted the reply.

The excitement was over. Head torches at the ready, all that remained was a long walk back on a track. At 11.45pm we arrived back at the car and it was a sheer coincidence that I said, 'If it takes until midnight'. We had broken our record yet again – 15.25 hours. Dave admitted that it had been the most testing and demanding day for him in every aspect, but was delighted at what we had achieved. I was proud of him. Another record was smashed that night as none of us had eaten lamb shanks and mashed potato followed by apple crumble at 1.30 in the morning. Carl had developed the habit of bringing his slow cooker to Scotland – he had no intention of living off beans on toast.

* * *

Some 30 hours after the Mam Sodhail epic we were back on the Munro trail. Sgurr nan Ceathreamhnan, Mullach na Dheiragain and An Socach. (A different An Socach to the one near Glenshee. Several mountains share the same name). Yet another marathon to look forward to, which for mere mortals would require an overnight stay of some kind. The Alltbeithe (Glen Affric) Hostel was perfectly placed. I'd made a booking several weeks prior to our visit due to its popularity, but also because Anita and I wanted to book one of the two private rooms. We got a private room and the men were in a dorm. The booking was for 20th May so shattered or not, that was when we would have to do the walk.

The alarm was set for 4.30am and at 6.15am we started the nine-mile walk to the hostel in order to reach the start of the actual route. Our rucksacks felt heavy. Not only was there the usual gear, including the now compulsory ice axes and crampons, but also sleeping bags and provisions for our evening meal and our breakfast. Carl was "volunteered" to carry the wine but he left the slow cooker behind. I'm sure our rucksacks were heavy but perhaps nearly two weeks of serious Munro bagging and eating evening meals after midnight made them appear heavier than they were.

We wanted to get to the hostel before 10.00am so a brisk pace was set. It was something I could have done without, but the only alternative was setting the alarm even earlier – no thanks. The weather was in a benevolent mood and we arrived at the hostel at 9.40am. Loch Ossian had felt remote with no roads and the railway station 20 minutes away, but Glen Affric takes first prize for remoteness. It's miles from civilisation with no telephone and no internet – absolute bliss. There were no "phone clones" staring at the screen on their smartphones oblivious of their surroundings and who they might be walking into.

A friendly welcome greeted us as Audrey appeared with a pot of tea. We were sitting outside sipping our tea in the sunshine glancing across at the River Affric without a thought for the three Munros we were about to tackle. Audrey seemed a little surprised at our plan to do all three but waved us off as she hung some washing out on what looked like an old bit of climbing rope. Ice axes and crampons were still with us as we could see the snow in the distance, but for the moment we were bathed in sunshine and dressed in the minimum amount of gear. I say minimum, but perhaps not. I had known people to wear less. In the dim and distant past a group of us were walking in the Lake District when we met a naked walker heading our way. Not THE naked rambler but a chap without clothes on. He had a rucksack, a pair of boots and was wearing spectacles. I felt sorry for him as we were well off the beaten track and the chances of him meeting a group of people must have been pretty slim. After perhaps the tenth person in our group passing him, I was told he put a pair of shorts on. I was near the front so never saw his shorts …

We'd only been going half an hour when I stopped in my tracks. There, just to the side of me was an adder. It was the first time I'd seen a snake and considering I don't like to watch snakes on TV, I was rather surprised that I wasn't frightened and found him fascinating. I think he was only a baby. Dave couldn't get the camera out quick enough so unfortunately little hissing Sid disappeared into the heather choosing not to have his photo taken.

We arrived at the bealach at 2,590ft (790 metres) along with the snow. "Chrysanthemum" – another mountain with a nickname – was to be the first Munro. There she was, covered in snow, with the snow extending all the way down the ridge that we would be taking to reach number two Munro. It wasn't long before the usual winter equipment came out. We'd gone from glorious weather to low cloud and poor visibility, but of course not an unusual phenomenon. I bet hissing Sid was happily curled up in the heather. We arrived at the summit in a whiteout. Perhaps Chrysanthemum found this amusing having watched us set off on a beautiful sunny day in the glen, to battening down the hatch. Dave was standing extremely close to what appeared to be a razor-sharp edge so I asked him to move away. He smiled and said that was our route off the mountain … wonderful. Peering over the edge I made out roughly where we were heading, down a narrow ridge with a boat-load of snow and atrocious visibility. Dave picked a way through and the lemmings duly followed.

Safely at the bottom of the ridge, Mullach na Dheiragain was the next port of call. Mullach had very little snow on him, but what he lacked in snow he more than made up for in numerous false tops and boulder fields. I digress a little. Ships are regarded as female, but I have no idea what gender mountains hold, if indeed they do. I feel most are male, with the odd exception holding female status. Mullach was male and a miserable old sod at that.

Enthusiasm had vanished with the snow and by the time we reached the summit a serious storm cloud was hovering in my head. Carl saved the day in the shape of a chewy sweet once known as an Opal Fruit. All meaningful conversation had long since passed but Anita and I gave the sweets our undivided attention and discussed tactics. Do you chew and it's over in an instant or can you find the willpower to cherish the moment and prolong the enjoyment? We turned round to see Carl and Dave more or less choking on their sweets, doubled over with laughter. What on earth was wrong with them? The penny dropped as we realised how their schoolboy "behind the bike shed" humour had kicked in. Four people in hysterics on top of a mountain over such childish humour was perhaps absurd, but the storm cloud in my head had gone. I shall never look an Opal Fruit in the face again without recalling that day. Enough of the hilarity, we still had the third Munro to visit.

It was a long way retracing our steps to Bealach nan Daoine. Dave headed past the loch of Coire nan Dearcag and back up to "bealach 2590". Our final goal of An Socach didn't have any snow on but once more it would be a case of going up and then back the same way. Going up to come down, to then go up again repeated several times in a day was a real test of mental endurance as much as physical. Crampons were abandoned at the bealach – anything to make life easier – and Dave left his rucksack. I was sticking with mine. Mhic Choinnich on the Isle of Skye may have been a distant memory, but once bitten twice shy. Sadly, An Socach only received a cursory visit before we retreated to the abandoned gear and down to the hostel, arriving just before 9pm. We'd been out 10.5 hours, plus the 3.5 hours getting to the hostel. No doubt we could have managed a further 3.5 hours to return to the car, but goodness knows what state we would have been in.

The atmosphere was warm and inviting as we walked through the door, with people chattering to one another and exchanging stories, a far cry from those phone clones out there in the other world. Audrey had been looking out for us through her binoculars and it seemed people were genuinely impressed with our sortie. However, when listening to what others had done, especially in view of their ages, we were the ones who were captivated. Dave seemed quite youthful in comparison. There were younger people staying of various nationalities. A gentleman told us that he had completed all the Munros some time ago but made a comment that stuck in my mind, 'It was like falling into a black hole when I finished'. I listened intently, unlike Dave who was absorbed by his wife. She was leaning over a table looking at a map to see where we had been. Her pert Dutch derriere had Dave mesmerised. Only after several short sharp kicks to his shins was the spell broken.

Our bottle of wine went down a treat but we did feel we'd earned it, and although the usual tinned baked beans and sausages had been heavy to carry in, I think one or two would have exchanged their freeze-dried meals for ours. I marvelled to see meals being prepared and cooked from scratch – one lady was busy peeling and chopping vegetables. That could be a chore at home, let alone in the middle of nowhere when you could be enjoying yourself. But perhaps she was.

The following morning we left the hostel and I enjoyed the leisurely walk back to the car. The same couldn't be said for poor Anita – her legs and feet had just about given up the ghost. We called at a shop on

the drive back to the cottage for such items as bread and milk. The men offered to go in as they could see neither Anita nor I were budging from the comfort of the car. Dave asked whether he should get one pint or two pints of milk, wholemeal or white bread, a small or large tub of butter. I found the questions irritating and ridiculously difficult to answer. 'Get what you want,' was the reply. I was tired, but my thoughts were with Chrysanthemum and hissing Sid. I resented stepping back into the real world which necessitated making such trivial decisions.

CHAPTER 15

BLACK HOLES AND BLACK DAYS

June and July 2015

The exceptionally strenuous days in April and May had paid unexpected dividends in the form of losing nearly half a stone in weight. And that was in spite of eating chocolate and drinking red wine. For long enough I had tried to stick to a diet and failed, but now the mountains had done it for me. So here was the opportunity to keep the weight off and perhaps be a tad more agile on the next round of Munros. More visits were planned in the summer months, and short of a major incident we were easily on track for 31st December.

I was more relaxed with the pressure of timescales a thing of the past, and yet a tinge of sadness was creeping in. It was June and we were on a steady day out of some eight hours. Having experienced so many mammoth days, a more normal excursion was seen as a luxury. The weather was good by our standards and there were no knee-trembling sections on this walk. So why on earth did I find myself fighting back the tears as I walked into yet another corrie? It occurred to me how precious the mountains were, but the end of this amazing adventure was in sight. My bubble was in its twilight years and in due course it would burst, tipping me into the Black Hole. Of course the mountains would still be there after 31st, but what of the adventure? I rationalised that a constructive outlook was required to this predicament and purposefully strode on, savouring every moment and admiring my mountain friends. I mustn't waste a minute or take the next hour for granted. It certainly worked, with one happy bunny hopping about the place and Dave wondering what I'd eaten for breakfast. This was not a one-off and became my default setting in amongst stepping out of my bubble world back into drab reality.

We were having a new bathroom fitted and, of course, the work over-ran. Visiting Scotland wasn't going to be cancelled but being such an impatient person, I wasn't prepared to delay the bathroom work until our return. So decisions were made hundreds of miles away about dark grey grout, light grey grout or perhaps even white grout. But then white grout could look "cheap and chatty" in view of the tiles I'd chosen. Exactly where did I want the toilet roll holder fixing? Dave couldn't see any problems. The tiler could select the grout and where else would you want a toilet roll holder, other than by the toilet. If only it was that simple. All phone calls were made either prior to heading into the mountains or afterwards. I wasn't going to abuse my Munros by discussing bathroom fittings while in their company. It was a similar situation when our new kitchen clashed with the winter mountaineering course in February 2013. I wasn't prepared to wait or miss out on either so a calculated gamble was taken with discussions en route to the north-west of Scotland. Finalising floor coverings – should it be laid at an angle or straight, what about inserts – and hoping they would interpret my requests as I pictured them in my head. Dave kept out of any decision making – he still thought 1980s tiles with little motifs on were acceptable. And anyway, what was wrong with the original kitchen? After all, it had only been in 25 years!

Most of our Munros in July were straightforward with a notable exception of Sgurr na Ciche, Garbh Chioch Mhor and Sgurr nan Coireachan situated to the north of Glen Dessary. They combine to make a route noted for its impressive scenic rocky ridge with Sgurr na Ciche possessing a picture book image of a pointy pyramid-shaped mountain. The three are rather secluded and the terrain is rugged so it could be bordering on the all too common epic classification. The threesome also had a neighbouring Munro, Sgurr Mor, which we needed to visit. The original plan was to climb the three and then visit Sgurr Mor another day. Had it been 2013 when I was new to this carry on perhaps that would have happened, but it was 2015 and a different Sue. I looked at the map and suggested we tag Sgurr Mor onto the three. Both walks started from the same place and sizeable chunks of the route would be repeated. Dave studied the map and agreed it would be possible. However, his statement was accompanied by a health warning. The three Munros would be a long and arduous walk, but adding a fourth would potentially verge on masochistic tendencies for the likes of us. We agreed on attempting four with my proviso to go clockwise leaving Sgurr Mor to the last. If everything went pear shaped it would be easier and logical to omit Mr Mor. It was amazing what good ideas blossomed after a nice meal, sitting in a comfortable chair. Carefully choosing which day to attempt this marathon could make all the difference between success and failure. So with all the forecasts saying the same, namely sunshine, not too hot and good visibility, a date was set – 14th July. The shorts nearly came out, but the prospect of midges swayed my decision back to trousers.

An early start was required, particularly as we had to drive to the far end of Loch Arkaig and we were based in Fort Augustus. I'd calculated a good hour to the start of the walk. Normally, my timings for driving were fairly accurate, but not on this occasion. Nearer the mark was 90 minutes, and an hour of that was spent doing an average of 12mph. The road along the loch was beautiful but single track. That in itself wasn't an issue, but the volume of traffic was a nightmare with contractors and temporary campsites for the workforce all over the place. It seemed they were installing some kind of pipeline. Add to that the ups and downs in the road itself – and to think people pay good money for such an experience at theme parks. Poor Petal was certainly put through her paces.

We started walking at 8.15am, later than hoped and to the accompaniment of midges. After the first hour a breeze had developed so our little friends vanished only to be replaced by boggy conditions underfoot. It was a good three hours of enduring bog hopping before there was any sign of improvement. We reached the bottom of a gully which led up to Feadan na Ciche. It was an enjoyable scramble but that was the last of any kind of pleasure. No midges, no bogs but the sun that had been shining had also gone, and we were left with the delights of low cloud and drizzle.

On reaching the summit of Sgurr na Ciche, waterproof trousers were in order as the drizzle became persistent rain. I was disappointed with the weather but for a change I was the one who remained positive. Dave was a little fed up while Anita was visibly displeased with the weather's performance. Luckily, the rain was vertical – after all it could have been worse and chosen a horizontal direction. I decided discretion was the better part of valour and remained silent with my observations. The inclement weather did make for trickier progress on wet slippery rock and the views, which I'm sure could be magnificent, were non-existent. We met two chaps heading towards us on this debatable exhilarating ridge walk. We'd met them earlier in the day before they headed anti-clockwise and they'd been shocked when they realised that we hoped to visit four Munros. Now in view of the rain and clag they asked if our plans had changed. We replied in the negative. They went on their way looking a little perplexed and shaking their heads, but wished us all the very best of luck.

We arrived at our second Munro, Garbh Chioch Mhor. Yet more slippery rocks and no views, although starting the descent to Bealach Coire nan Gall I sensed an improvement in the weather. The grey skies were now a lighter shade of grey and the rain was more akin to drizzle. 'It's just because we're losing height,' was Dave's response and Anita looked at me with a blank expression. How could I even think the weather was better!

We had to lose significant height to reach the start of the climb up onto the third Munro of the day, Sgurr nan Coireachan. Although I was in positive mode and pleased that my optimism towards the weather was proving right, I was tired. It was a mental battle which allowed progress and, not daring to look ahead, it was literally one foot in front of the other. I was oblivious to everything and only on arriving at the summit did I dare to look up. There was my reward – 360° views, sunshine and blue skies. A sandwich, a chocolate bar with a 20-minute rest and I felt fine. Bring on number four.

It had just turned 5pm so dare I ask the all-important question of was everyone happy to attempt the fourth Munro? I was rather careful with my wording. This had to be the glass half full approach. I pointed out that the sun was now shining, there were excellent views and we'd only been out just under nine hours. But more to the point we would then have a spare day to rest. I was given the green light. Off we toddled, but I kept looking back to see where we'd been in the clag. It looked splendid, Sgurr na Ciche in particular boastful in its seductive shape, and although Dave was in a much better frame of mind he quickly pointed out that he wouldn't be in any rush to return.

It can be misleading when you know there's only one more to do. As the crow flies there was no problem, but without the aid of wings there were several obstacles between us and Sgurr Mor, namely two tops to go over that didn't count on the scoreboard and which also meant losing height twice to regain it once more. I divided the journey into bite-size pieces in my little head. Psychologically, this seemed a better strategy, fooling the brain cells.

a) An Eag b) Sgurr Beag c) Sgurr Mor d) Return journey

Everyone enjoyed Eag and morale had taken a turn for the better because we could actually see where we were going. One down and just three more "bites" to go. It was a struggle on to Sgurr Beag, but even more of a mental effort when we had to lose height yet again before tackling Sgurr Mor.

The pills and potions came out before the final assault. My left knee was painful and I was already wearing a knee support so a cocktail of painkillers was selected. I offered a "fix" to Dave as I knew he was suffering, but as I expected he declined, so infuriatingly stubborn and quite irritating. It was a rarity for Dave to take any form of medication (fine on the basis that he remembered to suffer in silence) short of administering them as you would your pet Labrador: open their mouth, place on the back of the tongue, close the jaw, hold the mouth shut and rub their throat.

Anita led the way with Dave bringing up the rear. The summit was a damned sight further than any of us expected so a silent trudge was all we could manage. At just before 8pm we reached our destination. We were all weary but poor Dave was knackered and in pain. I hate using age as an excuse but perhaps his 66-year-old body was showing signs that it had seen better days. Me being a sprightly 59, no problem … I wish.

There was a chilly wind blowing and Anita seemed eager to push on, but much to my relief Dave was adamant we should rest and refuel right there. My painkillers had helped but not well enough and now my good knee was protesting. So I swapped the support from left to right. They would just have to take it in turns as I only possessed the one. I may have fooled the mind into easy manageable sections but there was no fooling the body. We had a steep descent on grassy slopes into Glen Kingie, one of the remotest glens in Scotland, then we had a river to cross. For once it was plain sailing and I still had a positive outlook on life. The same couldn't be said for Dave as in vain I tried my best to spur him on. It could have been more difficult if the snow had been down, or if it had been baking hot, so really, we were lucky. But Dave was having none of it.

We'd come down into the glen, now we needed to go back up the other side before we could start our last descent into Glen Dessary and pick up the track that would lead us back to long-lost Petal. We encountered yet more bog. The remaining daylight faded with each squelch we made. I genuinely felt for Dave as he strove to find the least boggy route, but with limited success. Perhaps it was a case of a bog too far when he shouted across to me, 'I'm not doing these f*****g mountains ever again!' Right, OK, that's cleared that up. Personally, I thought it hadn't been that bad, but there you go. We were reunited with Petal in the car park at twenty minutes after midnight – 16 hours after leaving and the first time we'd returned on a different day from when we'd started. It was a beautiful starlit night but sadly we weren't at our best to appreciate it. The relief was palpable, but there was the small issue of driving back. Dave kindly offered to drive, but I knew he was whacked, so I drove. I cheerily pointed out a hidden benefit that we'd overlooked; this interminable road wouldn't have to be visited ever again. But I was the only one upbeat.

The rollercoaster road kept me wide awake. There were no problems with workmen and their vehicles, just the wildlife to watch out for. Of course the ups and downs still required negotiating and on the ups the headlights were only useful for tracking low flying aircraft. I was fine until we left the wiggly road and joined normal tarmac. My eyes were like organ stops, looking but not seeing. Needs must and apologies to Dave and Anita but the air conditioning would have to be set to cold and just to be on the safe side I needed noise. Fleetwood Mac blasted away as we drove along, although at that hour there was nobody about to disturb. Just before arriving back in Fort Augustus Anita informed us she would not be cooking our meal that night/morning. Why would you not want to start cooking at 1.45am and after four Munros. Can't get the staff, eh!

At 2.15am we flopped into bed with coffee and biscuits, just 21 hours after the alarm had beeped.

CHAPTER 16

PENSIVE AND PENULTIMATE

September and October 2015

We had nine weeks respite before the penultimate visit to Scotland. Initially, this came as some physical relief but also allowed us to catch up on household tasks. This would normally be a pain in the butt but I felt some sense of satisfaction regaining control of situations. I like gardening to a degree, but when left unattended it fast became a chore. I relented and allowed the weeds to stay. They were in full bloom, quite pretty, and it's a person's perspective on what is or is not a weed. I watched "Gardeners' World" with a feeling of guilt, so a solution was found and I avoided watching a few episodes.

Sadly, I became aware that the garden wasn't the only aspect of my life that I'd neglected. Close friends who meant so much to me had been overlooked, my brother's birthday was totally dismissed and a credit card bill had been forgotten into the bargain. If we were in company and the topic of conversation didn't revolve around mountains we switched off in a very short space of time. We had a funeral to attend of a lady who was dear to me and had been there throughout my life. It happened to clash with a planned Munro-bagging week and although we managed to fulfil both I do remember my initial reaction was panic at the thought of having to abort the Munros. There were weeks when I didn't find the time to phone my friends. A close friend likened me to a juggler. I was trying to spin several plates on sticks, running from one to another to keep them spinning but not always succeeding. It made me take stock of myself and I wasn't sure I liked what I saw in the mirror. I was passionate about my life away from reality, and the bubble worlds I had come to love and cherish were addictive. However, one day I would have to recognise that I couldn't live in a Peter Pan world. I was very lucky that everyone accepted my apologies and stood by me. That's when you know what a good friend is.

By early September we were chomping at the bit, eager to be back in Scotland and looking forward to our fortnight in the West Highlands. Nine Munros were planned for the first week and 10 in the second week, leaving Fionn Bheinn for 31st December. We'd become slightly paranoid in the week leading up to our visit. We were so near to our target, but frightened of the unexpected. Dave had recently bought a new rope and went practising his climbing skills. Before he set off I told him to take care, but at the same time reminded him that we had a challenge to complete in a matter of weeks' time.

We were in one piece as we left North Yorkshire on 19th September 2015. Packing, including six large boxes of groceries and a cool bag, had become second nature. This was the most time-efficient procedure because there was no time to go shopping once we were in Scotland. Replenishing items such as milk and bread was squeezed in on a rest day. Despite a cavernous boot on a Ford Mondeo we also managed to fill the back seats. It had only taken three years to perfect the technique and perhaps I overdosed on spreadsheets, but they made life so much easier.

Our first week in North Ballachulish (once again) was open house, so a few friends were joining us. Anita would be missing the first two days due to her eldest daughter's wedding. As much as Anita wanted to be bagging Munros, her daughter's wedding had to take priority. Carl would be joining us in the second week but couldn't manage both weeks. He'd run out of holiday entitlement and was already taking unpaid leave.

It became apparent that we viewed the mountains and our days out in quite a different light to normal people. On returning to the cottage our friends would watch the news, chat about things in general with only a few minutes spent talking about where we had been and what was planned for the following day. This was quite alien to us. Our conversations revolved around Munros, looking at maps, checking driving times to the start of a walk, where to park and possible routes. When we were out in the mountains, if we'd aborted reaching a summit just because we felt tired, we'd be less than pleased and yet some of our friends wouldn't have given it a second thought. I would have felt exactly the same not that many moons ago, so if I'm honest our interest had become obsessional.

Karen, a very close friend of mine, once commented that she didn't like the long walk in to get to a mountain. It was Beinn Sgulaird, which is not exactly known for its inaccessibility. As for false summits, she would state in no uncertain terms that they were taking her beyond her threshold.

Although false summits were an annoyance, little frogs leaping out of the undergrowth totally freaked Karen. More than once she screamed out loud, much to the consternation of others on the mountain who presumed there had been an accident. I had to explain to one passing gentleman that it had only been a "frog alert". However, by the end of the week Karen showed considerable interest in listing the mountains she'd climbed. Her partner, Damien, who was definitely from the anti-tick establishment, was less than enamoured at the news.

We completed the nine Munros as planned and moved on to another cottage for the second week. Our friends headed south and it was just the four of us on the Munro trail. We moved slightly further north close to Banavie for our penultimate week when Carl had joined us. The cottage was an experience in itself with access on a dirt track through a 200-year-old tunnel that had the Caledonian Canal running above it. First impressions weren't favourable. There were some rather ramshackle old buildings, a rusty old 1970s car, hens wandering about the place and the cottage in amongst it all. How looks can be deceiving and little did I know I would be eating a large slice of humble pie before the end of the week.

It may have felt special as we were on the home straight, but it was no easier. We had the advantage of good weather, which made it less painful when the alarm went off at 6.30am and it was still dark outside. For someone who isn't a morning person this ritual was still difficult to accept. We all had our own routines and foibles. Mine was keeping a low profile by taking a couple of slices of toast back to the bedroom with few words uttered, the rucksack having been packed the night before. Carl and Anita had learned in the first year not to strike up a conversation with me. How anyone can leap out of bed, start chattering and then proceed to cheerily pack their rucksack beggars belief. We also had different ambient temperature settings for the central heating. Carl was a 15°C man, we were 20°C and Anita was closer to 25°C. Windows were surreptitiously opened and closed with thermostats "accidentally" being knocked up and down. The dishwasher was another learning curve. I wouldn't contemplate booking a property without one so I certainly couldn't see the point of hand washing items. When we were at home everything went in whether it was dishwasher proof or not. Anita realised she'd been wasting time for many years by being rather too selective on what went in a dishwasher and became rather more laid back about the contents. Carl's little quirk would be to bring his own kitchen knives and his slow-cooker. He enjoyed cooking and seemed at a loss without his top of the range knives. Little did I know they shouldn't be placed in a dishwasher, so of course when Carl discovered that was exactly where they had been, I was not flavour of the month. You see, until you live under the same roof with someone you have no idea that your way of doing things is not the same as others.

It had become noticeable that it now took considerably longer to prepare my feet prior to putting my socks on. A fabric (adhesive knit) was placed on a couple of toes, foam padding on the underside of my feet, one piece of moleskin dressing on one foot where my orthotic insoles caused friction, anti-inflammatory gel rubbed over my ankles and finally a gel support on each ankle. The knee support was one of the few items not classified as compulsory, but then the painkillers gulped down after breakfast may have camouflaged that niggle. Mind over matter, age is but a number. To be fair, it wasn't just me, so extra time was allowed in a morning for the various procedures. Only Carl could get dressed without the burden of a mobile chemist shop in tow.

* * *

We had some wonderful days completing the 10 Munros on our list. Our longest day was a mere 11 hours when we were in the Grey Corries near Spean Bridge. Stob Choire Claurigh, Stob Coire an Laoigh and Sgurr Choinnich Mor were the targets. These weren't an epic, but were a challenging spectacular route with an airy ridge. The last one was rather a mental challenge as much as physical. It was out on a limb with not the easiest terrain to negotiate and involved losing a considerable amount of height before climbing once more. However, with near perfect conditions, where else would I rather be? Nowhere was the answer. By early evening we were heading down, but I loathed leaving the mountains. Now it was near the end of the challenge they seemed to be all the more special.

Mistakes were rarely made in bad conditions, but we all seemed laid back as we aimed for a dam. Heading down a rather steep and slippery slope we arrived at the dam wall. From a distance it had looked quite innocuous, but now up close and personal it was far from inviting. Some dam walls have a walkway, but not this one. This one had round coping stones finished off with a light covering of slime and moss. Rather than keep my thoughts to myself I erred on the side of caution and shared my thoughts. 'Dave, don't even think about it.' I hurriedly pulled a copy of the route details out of my rucksack. "We" had overlooked, "aim towards the dam but cross the burn a little way upstream prior to the dam". Thankfully, the water was low and it only required perhaps 100 yards of backtracking. It appeared that several people had made the same mistake as there was a fair-sized trod both heading to the dam and then back along the stream. I always say you should never drop your guard in Scotland because it's not over until "the fat lady sings".

There were some decent forest tracks to walk on which led to an old dismantled railway track and then the car park. Walking through the forest was enchanting, particularly in one section where a real chill in the air was quite noticeable. The grass was covered with a string of dew-speckled spiders' webs with Christmas trees lining each side of the track. The sky was aglow with different hues of yellow, pink, blue and purple as the sun began to set. Walt Disney couldn't have conjured up a more magical setting. Dave was in overdrive, which seemed criminal in such a place, but I was going to savour the experience and went at my own pace.

We arrived back at the car, this time Anita's. Driving to the start of this walk up Corriechoille meant a fair old distance on a track far more suited to a 4 x 4 vehicle and as Anita's car fitted the bill, we let Petal have the day off. It was rather nice for me to sit in the back and not bother about driving. A rarity, but it was through choice. Being driven down the bumpy track I could admire a blanket of mist hovering above the fields with the sun's glow as its backdrop. Autumn has always been my favourite season and today had provided the evidence of why it is a special time of the year.

Dave and I were relaxed, looking forward to the following day off, Anita and Carl less so. In fact, Carl didn't have much to say at all. Anita had missed out on some of the Munros we'd done in the first week due to her daughter's wedding so had decided to forgo the day off and had persuaded Carl to join her on another day of Munro bagging. This in addition to having bagged a Munro on the day we transferred cottages. We couldn't understand Anita's logic because she wasn't working to a specific deadline and already had problems with her knees. Dave and I went to bed looking forward to the forthcoming lazy day. I prefer to have curtains partially drawn back and that particular night was no exception. Lying in bed I could see the silhouette of Ben Nevis with a backdrop of countless stars and the moon's shiny face smiling down on Planet Earth. I didn't want to sleep and miss the spectacle. I nudged Dave, but the response was a grunt. Oh well, his loss as he would say. A little while later

I could see flickering lights moving down the mountain. Either somebody had misjudged timings or had encountered problems, but hopefully it was an intentional descent in darkness. From the comfort of my bed and snuggled under a duvet, this was a priceless display and not to be missed. The next thing I remember was the sound of the door closing as Anita and Carl left to go Munro bagging.

* * *

Dave and I had a leisurely breakfast. The owners of the property came across to deliver freshly laid eggs, escorted by their three Labradors and the hens which had produced the said eggs. They were a lovely couple who appeared to have given up the rat race and were running a small holding alongside the self-catering cottage and a B&B. It no longer mattered about the outside; I loved my new environment. The crowning glory was a two-minute walk from the doorstep and wonderful navigation on my part. Turn left after passing the pigs, through the gate and there was a shingle beach where the River Lochy flowed. With clear blue skies and temperatures in keeping with the Med', we had definitely stepped into paradise.

Several hours later Anita and Carl returned, tired, hot and sweaty. Even Anita had felt the heat so it must have been hot. We explained that we too had experienced problems, and that trying to eat ice cream before it melted was really quite stressful.

* * *

It was the last day and the penultimate Munro, Gulvain. Back to more usual weather: cloud. However, it was dry with little wind and we could just about see the tops of the mountains, except for Gulvain. Unsurprisingly, Anita was finding it incredibly difficult to place one foot in front of the other so a very steady pace was set and even then we would have to stop and allow her to catch up.

Dave and I were on our own for a while so I took the opportunity to clear the air about my participation in route finding and how I felt. Dave was genuinely concerned and hadn't realised how upset and hurt I'd been on a previous outing. We were returning from Sgorr Dhonuill and Sgorr Dhearg. I'd been trying to be helpful with the navigation but because my information had been gleaned from a different source, Dave wasn't paying any attention and was getting quite stroppy. So much so that I threw the details at him which he duly threw back at me. Anita and Carl were perhaps taking imaginary bets as to who would kill who first. I vowed to keep my nose out of it and promised silence. I kept my word even when we reached a track where I felt sure we needed to turn right, but Dave carried straight on. I was correct, but a promise was a promise so I remained silent. Before you lecture me on my childish actions, I will point out that we were out of the mountains so not in any danger. It just meant a longer way back to the car. Sometimes you just have to cut off your nose to spite your face and perhaps it did make Dave think.

Now where were we? Yes, heading towards Gulvain. A chap passed us on a bicycle as this was one of the many mountains you could pedal in part of the way – if you could ride a bike. Anita was decidedly shattered but even Dave was showing signs of weariness. He happened to stumble on a loose rock in the smallest of burns and down he went. Dave rarely slipped on such things – that was my domain – and there was a slight pause before he got to his feet again. Oh no, would Gulvain be abandoned? That obsessive selfish side had surfaced again and I went on to suggest that if nothing was broken, painkillers would get him to the top. As we gained height the clouds bowed their heads to meet us. Visibility was non-existent. As Gulvain is a "there and back the same way", we bumped into our bicycle chap. It turned out he was on his third round of Munros with just 30 left to do. He said it would definitely be his last round as his knees were in a sad state of affairs. Once again it's more or less impossible to explain to a non-Munro bagger why people allow and accept that their bodies will be abused. I suppose it's like any sport when you think about it.

There was the summit peering out of the mist – number 281. We'd taken some Prosecco and Carl and Anita had brought a chocolate cake for a mini celebration. It was a shame the clag was down, but the day was just as special. What on earth would it be like on 31st December? I allowed myself to switch my phone on for a brief moment in order to text a few people of our whereabouts. Oh dear; were my standards beginning to slip?

Coming down was easy unless you were called Anita. She may have been steady going up but coming down was more difficult and painful. Even when we reached flat ground it didn't seem to help and Dave was getting slower by the minute, doing his best to preserve his knees. Carl and I chuckled about being out with the local OAP group and debated whether a Zimmer frame would fit in a rucksack.

More treats were in store for us during our evening meal. A bottle of champagne and another cake appeared, courtesy of Anita and Carl. It was touching when Carl gave a little speech saying how he wouldn't have missed the experience for the world and both he and Anita felt privileged to have been able to accompany us on our mission. You can never tell how an idea will work out. At the outset we had pictured the two of us roving the glens and mountains of Scotland on our own. Even when we invited Anita and Carl, neither of us envisaged the shape the adventure would take. Invariably three people, quite often four. In fact, looking at the tick list, only a handful of Munros were climbed on our own and I haven't written about them. They were enjoyable times, when we seemed very relaxed and argued very little. But perhaps that doesn't make for entertaining reading. However, it goes to prove that you can take a different direction and sometimes discover even better times. Looking back, we wouldn't have wanted it any other way.

CHAPTER 17

FIONN BHEINN, THE FINAL CURTAIN

December 2015

It was the countdown to the last Munro, Fionn Bheinn. The interval between Gulvain and 31st December seemed too large but we had built in an allowance in the event that there had been problems along the way. The accommodation had been booked way back in May 2013 with Hogmanay being a popular time in Scotland. Fionn Bheinn hadn't been a worry, but the planning was akin to a military operation. If everything went to plan there would be 20 people on the final summit. There was a considerable variation in abilities from the hardened few accustomed to the Scottish mountains to those who were more at home enjoying a leisurely stroll in the Yorkshire Dales.

So why or how was Fionn Bheinn chosen to bring the curtain down on the challenge? The likes of Ben Lomond and Schiehallion are very popular choices, being not as far for people to travel and are mountains that have substantial paths leading to the respective summits. My choice was down to Mr Moran. I had spoken about the challenge while I was on the snowhole adventure in 2013 when I had the princely sum of 50 Munros under my belt. I wouldn't go as far as to say that Martin didn't believe I was capable of bagging the Munros within the timescale, but I sensed some scepticism in his voice when I mentioned I had Beinn Sgritheall in mind for my final one. He asked if our friends were mountaineers. Of course that was not the case, and I think he knew very well that would be my answer. My limited knowledge of the Scottish mountains had prompted me to query his comment, to be told that on 31st December, in the depths of winter, Beinn Sgritheall would more than likely require mountaineering skills. It was Martin who suggested that Fionn Bheinn might be more suitable for the occasion. Beinn Sgritheall was one of the few Munros Dave and I had visited on our own on a beautiful autumnal day. We knew exactly what

Martin was talking about when we discovered the top section was steep and even in perfect conditions required care.

There were many spreadsheets flying about in the build-up to 31st December and Dave reminded me that I would have to delegate some tasks. That was easier said than done when you're a natural control freak. However, there were plenty of offers to help transport 100 bottles of wine.

Achnasheen is a tiny hamlet north-east of Lochcarron and 40 miles west of Inverness. It's also the starting point for Fionn Bheinn. The Ledgowan Lodge Hotel was the only hotel and was the perfect place for our group. In addition to its location they let it out on a self-catering basis over Christmas and New Year which was perfect for us. Well, it was perfect after I managed to find a lady who provided catering services. Cooking for six is quite an undertaking in my book so cooking for 20 people was totally out of the question. I would even go so far as to say that the Cuillin is a less daunting prospect than feeding "the five thousand."

My last day at work was 18th December when my work colleagues presented me with a variety of gifts to mark my forthcoming milestone birthday. They had been so generous. A cake, a bouquet of flowers, a rather nice bottle of red wine and a gift voucher (for walking gear), but the jewel in the crown was a framed oil painting of Fionn Bheinn painted by the man I work with. Steve regards himself as a very average artist, but he's the only one who thinks so. Everyone else says he's brilliant. All the other gifts were lovely, but the picture was priceless. Apparently Steve's wife had remarked on the slightly moody sky portrayed in the picture and wondered why Steve hadn't painted a more cheerful blue sky. Steve knew I "did" moody and atmospheric.

Time stood still over the Christmas period and we became worried about possible illness or injury while watching every weather forecast we could find. We had every faith in getting to Achnasheen, but some of our friends were a tad nervous, feeling that the north-west of Scotland was a million miles away. We did our best to reassure them that it was an easy drive and that snow ploughs were part and parcel of the scenery should they be required, which is more than can be said for down here.

* * *

At last, 29th December arrived and we were on our final journey. I was like a big kid on my way to see Santa Claus. I doubt many people would describe visiting Stirling service station as a poignant moment in their lives and it seemed fitting that it was just Dave and me in the car. Ten minutes before we got to Achnasheen the nerves kicked in and I had a touch of the Cuillin Collywobbles. Had I forgotten anything, would everyone be happy, what if the Ledgowan didn't live up to expectation, would people cancel at the last minute? I aimed to arrive at 3pm but it was 2.55pm. As we walked through the door of the Ledgowan I was taken aback at what greeted me. Tasteful Christmas decorations adorned the wood panelled reception area, a log fire was burning, boxes of chocolates and nuts placed on the coffee tables and there was Carl sitting in a wing-backed chair, smiling. The feel of the place was so homely and welcoming. Why was I worried as this was everything I dreamed of? Twelve were staying the first night with the remaining eight joining us the following day. The nerves disappeared as people started to arrive. They were so impressed with the place and those of us who had travelled on the Tuesday had beautiful weather making the journey a pleasure. The same couldn't be said for the others the following day.

Snow had always been a concern but torrential rain had never entered our heads. Diane and Glynn, our sun-loving friends, contacted me to say there had been a landslide near Garve 20 miles away from the hotel. The road was blocked and it had also impacted on the Inverness–Kyle of Lochalsh Railway. While they were making further enquiries, so did I. The only alternative route would entail a huge detour and would more than likely have flooding issues. An awful thought struck me about our lady who was cooking for us as she lived in the vicinity of Garve. If she couldn't get through, beans on toast x 20 may not be what people had in mind. After a couple of hours all was well as the minor landslide had been resolved and the road had re-opened. However, the next issue for two couples who had set off later was the M74 had been closed due to flooding. Why was I panicking? This didn't matter a jot to our loyal friends. They were taking whatever diversions necessary and, literally, come hell or high water they were going to get through. Some had been travelling over 10 hours.

* * *

Thursday 31st December, the day I had been waiting for these past three years. It was my birthday, but it was Fionn Bheinn that was in my thoughts. That was until I went down for breakfast. Fairies had been a feature on several trips. They polished rivers and sprinkled snow, and now they had visited the Ledgowan and covered the place in 60th birthday banners and balloons. What a lovely start to the day.

It's hard trying to get 20 people together and ready at the appointed hour and is possibly similar to herding sheep. You think you have them all and then one wanders off closely followed by its mate. Before you know where you are you've lost the lot. Today it worked surprisingly well. All 20 of us set off on a cold, frosty morning with three variations of Susan/Sue, and a Martyn B and a Martin I, should you get confused later on. The weather could have been an issue. What would we have done if the conditions had been dire? A handful would have been capable of tackling the mountain, but not everyone. We could have delayed until 1st January but I had set my heart on 31st December. However, all our friends had travelled hundreds of miles to share the moment. Fortunately, that scenario was now immaterial and one less thing to worry about.

All the days, months and years of dreaming about this day I had pictured we would be the only ones on Fionn Bheinn, so it came as some surprise to see another group heading in the same direction. Panic, now what do I do? Of course I could do nothing and they would be made welcome to join the celebrations. No sooner had that issue been resolved before another problem entered my head. What if they were celebrating their last Munro? With my best positive head on, I concluded we could celebrate together … if we had to.

Carl had been placed in charge of the group and for once it would be good for Dave not to have the responsibility of leading. This was a straightforward route in the good weather we were enjoying, but accommodating the wide variety of abilities and speed was not that simple. Two or three had been losing sleep prior to the event wondering whether they would manage, and no matter how many times I tried to reassure them, I knew they were anxious. It was a good job I heeded Martin's (Martin M) advice on the choice of mountain. The higher we went the sunnier it became, and with a covering of snow it was picture perfect. As a consequence of taking the walk at a very steady pace we were considerably slower than the other group who had been to the summit and disappeared before we even got there. I had worried for nothing.

We must have been 75% of the way up with nearly all the hard work over and most of the group ahead of us, when one of our friends had a breathing problem. Susan "I" had been determined to give Fionn Bheinn her best shot even though she normally enjoyed walks of a much steadier nature. She had done marvellously well, and with a determined approach she was well on the way to finding success. She stopped and used her inhaler several times but to no avail. Her husband, (Martin I) was with her trying to reassure her, but all she could say was how sorry she was for the problem she was causing. She was fully aware her husband had his heart set on reaching the top in the way she had hoped. The unintentional pressure exacerbated the symptoms so we needed to ease the tension for her to relax a little. With much reassurance from various people and me making some ridiculous remarks (which of course came easily) such as likening Fionn Bheinn to Everest and if it meant taking two steps then stopping for a breather, well that's what we would do. I pointed out that we had often taken 15 hours or more to complete a Munro and while Fionn Bheinn was not renowned for being a lengthy day, we could always buck the trend. The ice was broken as we started chuckling, Dave took her rucksack then Susan relaxed and started to recover. I hadn't bargained for such an event so obviously there was a loophole in my planning.

Ten minutes later and everyone was at the summit waiting for Dave and me. It tended to be overlooked that not only was it my last Munro, but it was also Dave's final one and without him I would never have been there. We had purposely hung back to take it all in and I was feeling quite numb. Just before the last person left us to join the throng, they commented what an amazing adventure we must have had and this was the end of an era. Total meltdown. I looked up at Dave with tears running down my face saying I didn't want it to end and by touching the trig point my bubble would burst. Dave said nothing, his eyes were red as he took my hand. Hand in hand we headed for the summit. Some of our friends formed a guard of honour using trekking poles while others cheered and clapped. A few more steps and we touched the trig point together. Hugs and kisses were in gay abandon and one or two others also had watery eyes.

The mighty snow-covered mountains of the Torridons could be seen as Loch Fannich sparkled in the sunlight. Diane said she could understand a little of why the mountains meant so much to me. Numerous photos were taken and then what seemed like an endless number of champagne bottles appeared from various rucksacks. Dave and I had just completed our last Munro and Susan, the lady who had been poorly, had just climbed her first Munro. It goes to prove you can just about attempt anything if your heart is set on it.

Two men were approaching us. What perfect timing, and perhaps they would be kind enough to take a group photo. Of course we would reward them with a plastic cup of champagne. They were more than happy to oblige, but as I started to tell them the story of who we were and where we'd come from, they smiled and said they already knew about us from Martin Moran. They were on one of his courses and had a day off. It had been suggested they might find a party on the top of Fionn Bheinn.

It was time to leave the summit. However, we asked if people would leave without us so we could spend some time on our own. Of course, Fionn Bheinn had been chosen for its simplicity but she was now up there with a few more special mountains and my goodness, she had treated us well. Then we started to make our way down. The group had split into two with some choosing to head straight back but others wanted to extend their time in the mountains and savour the day for a little while longer. We chose the longer option and as we walked away from the summit I stopped to look back. With nobody on her summit she seemed at ease now that we had left her in peace, our footprints in the snow the only sign we had disturbed her. I had come a long way in more ways than one since the day I walked round Crummock Water. How true it is that it's not the destination that matters, but the journey. Dave took a photo looking back up the mountain. It was the perfect image that Steve had captured in the painting.

We caught up with the others and ambled back to the Ledgowan. I think we were all in a slightly melancholy mood, but there was no time for sadness as we walked through the door. The direct group were there with glasses of champagne at the ready. If alcohol was required you could guarantee that our friends Stephen and Susan would be there to help! However, they were also excellent at setting a beautiful dining table. Not only did we have champagne but an amazing celebration cake appeared. Two figures sculpted in fondant icing on top of a mountain, two little rucksacks, two ice axes and a sign reading Fionn Bheinn. I had a feeling a good friend by the name of Pat had a large part to play in that surprise. Earlier in the day I'd had another surprise. It was a voucher for a trial flying lesson in a helicopter that included flying over Glencoe – brilliant. My friends apologised as they'd tried in vain to arrange for me to be winched into a helicopter. Bless them, and how thoughtful.

There was a lull in the celebrations before the evening events kicked off. Dave dusted off his funeral/wedding/christening suit and the high heels came out along with a new dress. Both were a rarity, but it was good to go the whole hog. There were two specific highlights still to look forward to. One of our friends Martyn "B" specialised in creating film/slide shows set to music. We'd provided the ingredients and suspected that the end results would far exceed our hopes. The other highlight also concerned a Martin but this time Martin Moran. For the past 12 months he'd said that he'd call to say hello, and perhaps he was a little curious to see what format the film show would take. We appreciated he was a busy man and we were just two of his many clients, but it was because of Martin the challenge was born and turned my life upside down. Dave and I cannot thank him enough for changing our lives for the better. I needn't have worried as neither Martyn nor Martin let me down. Dave said I was worrying for nothing, yet again. Martin arrived and surprised us by kindly presenting each of us with a tartan scarf. We were thrilled he had found the time to join us.

Martyn produced a wonderful, amusing yet moving film show. And something quite unusual happened. Earlier in the evening I had given a little speech and asked people to raise their glass in remembrance of our late friend Con. Perhaps he had been looking down on us at the top of Fionn Bheinn. Not even Dave knew what I was going to say and I had no idea how Martyn would end the film show … Martyn had included a group photograph with a superimposed image of Con. We were stunned. Con had kept his word; he told me he would be there for my last Munro.

I hope you've enjoyed a glimpse into some of my memorable moments even though my words have not done justice to the mountains. I'm not too sure how to end this story or if I even want to end the tale. By finishing the last chapter the book will close the curtain on my adventure. Will that be when I find the Black Hole in a world where bubbles don't exist? Only time will tell. In just a few more seconds the keyboard will fall silent as my story finally ends. But I truly believe that my memories and my mountains will be with me until I take my last breath.

Bloody Marvellous!

CHAPTER 18

LIST OF MUNROS IN DATE ORDER

DATE	NUMBER	MUNRO
09/08/1998	1	Cairn Gorm
	2	Ben Macdui
	3	Beinn Alligin Sgurr Mhor
	4	Beinn Alligin Tom na Gruagaich
	5	Liathach Spidean a'Choire Leith
	6	Liathach Mullach an Rathain
	7	An Teallach Bidean a'Ghlas Thuill
	8	An Teallach Sgurr Fiona
	9	Beinn Eighe Spidean Coire nan Clach
	10	Beinn Eighe Ruadh-stac Mor
	11	Slioch
	12	A'Mhaighdean
	13	Meall a'Chrasgaidh
	14	Sgurr Mor
	15	Beinn Liath Mhor Fannaich
	15	Aonach Eagach Sgorr nam Fiannaidh
	17	Aonach Eagach Meall Dearg
	18	Ben Nevis
	19	Carn Mor Dearg
	20	Buachaille Etive Mor Stob Dearg
	21	Cona' Mheall
	22	Beinn Dearg
	23	Sgurr nan Clach Geala

	24	Sgurr nan Each
	25	Bidean Nam Bian
	26	Stob Coire Sgreamhach
	27	A'Chailleach
	28	Sgurr Breac
	29	An Coileachan
	30	Meall nan Ceapraichean
	31	Eididh nan Clach Geala
	32	Ruadh Stac Mor
	33	The Saddle
	34	Sgurr Fhuaran
	35	Sgurr na Ciste Duibhe
	36	Sgurr na Carnach
	37	Druim Shionnach
	38	Aonach air Chrith
	39	Maol Chinn-dearg
	40	Ben Wyvis
	41	Bla Bheinn (Blaven)
	42	Sgurr nan Eag
	43	Sgurr nan Gillean
	44	Beinn Narnain
	45	Beinn Ime
	46	Bruach na Frithe
	47	Am Basteir
	48	Sgurr na Banachdich
12/09/2012	49	Sgurr Dearg (Inaccessible Pinnacle)
12/02/2013	50	Sgurr na Sgine
03/03/2013	51	An Caisteal
03/03/2013	52	Beinn a'Chroin
04/03/2013	53	Beinn Tulaichean
04/03/2013	54	Cruach Ardrain
06/04/2013	55	Ben More Assynt

06/04/2013	56	Conival
07/04/2013	57	Ben Klibreck
08/04/2013	58	Ben Hope
02/05/2013	59	Ciste Dhubh
04/05/2013	60	Creag a'Mhaim
05/05/2013	61	Carn na Caim
05/05/2013	62	A'Bhuidheanach Bheag
06/05/2013	63	Meall Chuaich
19/05/2013	64	Meall Buidhe
19/05/2013	65	Luinne Bheinn
20/05/2013	66	Ladhar Bheinn
10/06/2013	67	Creag Meagaidh
10/06/2013	68	Stob Poite Coire Ardair
10/06/2013	69	Carn Liath
11/06/2013	70	Ben Chonzie
04/07/2013	71	Ben Vorlich
04/07/2013	72	Stuc a'Chroin
05/07/2013	73	Beinn a'Ghlo – Carn nan Gabhar
05/07/2013	74	Beinn a'Ghlo- Braigh Coire Chruinn-bhalgain
05/07/2013	75	Beinn a'Ghlo- Carn Liath
06/07/2013	76	Carn a'Chlamain
07/07/2013	77	Schiehallion
21/07/2013	78	Carn nan Gobhar
21/07/2013	79	Sgurr na Lapaich
21/07/2013	80	An Riabhachan
21/07/2013	81	An Socach
11/08/2013	82	Beinn Chabhair
12/08/2013	83	Ben More
12/08/2013	84	Stob Binnein
13/08/2013	85	Ben Lomond
01/09/2013	86	Carn Gorm

01/09/2013	87	Meall Garbh
01/09/2013	88	Carn Mairg
01/09/2013	89	Creag Mhor
02/09/2013	90	Meall Glas
02/09/2013	91	Sgiath Chuil
03/09/2013	92	Stuchd an Lochain
03/09/2013	93	Meall Buidhe
05/09/2013	94	Meall Greigh
05/09/2013	95	Meall Garbh
05/09/2013	96	An Stuc
05/09/2013	97	Ben Lawers
06/09/2013	98	Beinn Ghlas
06/09/2013	99	Meall Corranaich
06/09/2013	100	Meall a'Choire Leith
06/09/2013	101	Meall nan Tarmachan
22/09/2013	102	Maol Chean-dearg
23/09/2013	103	Beinn Liath Mhor
23/09/2013	104	Sgorr Ruadh
24/09/2013	105	Sgurr an Doire Leathain
24/09/2013	106	Sgurr an Lochain
24/09/2013	107	Creag nan Damh
26/09/2013	108	Sgurr Choinnich
26/09/2013	109	Sgurr a'Chaorachain
27/09/2013	110	Moruisg
29/09/2013	111	Sgurr Eilde Mor
29/09/2013	112	Binnein Beag
29/09/2013	113	Binnean Mor
29/09/2013	114	Na Gruagaichean
30/09/2013	115	An Gearanach Ring of Steall
30/09/2013	116	Stob Coire a'Chairn
30/09/2013	117	Am Bodach
30/09/2013	118	Sgurr a'Mhaim

01/10/2013	119	Aonach Beag
01/10/2013	120	Aonach Mor
02/10/2013	121	Stob Dubh
02/10/2013	122	Stob Coire Raineach
04/10/2013	123	Stob na Broige
13/10/2013	124	Beinn Sgritheall
14/10/2013	125	Beinn Fhada
14/10/2013	126	a'Ghlas-bheinn
30/11/2013	127	Ben Vane
01/12/2013	128	Beinn Bhuidhe
02/12/2013	129	Ben Vorlich
30/12/2013	130	Sgairneach Mhor
30/12/2013	131	Beinn Udlamain
31/12/2013	132	Geal-charn
02/01/2014	133	Carn Dearg
03/01/2014	134	Geal Charn
04/01/2014	135	A'Chailleach
04/01/2014	136	Carn Sgulain
02/02/2014	137	Creag Leacach
04/02/2014	138	Driesh
04/02/2014	139	Mayar
06/02/2014	140	An Socach
07/02/2014	141	Carn an Tuirc
07/02/2014	142	Cairn of Claise
07/02/2014	143	Glas Maol
09/03/2014	144	Beinn Dearg
10/03/2014	145	Sgor Gaoith
11/03/2014	146	Bynack More
11/03/2014	147	Beinn a'Chlachair
11/03/2014	148	Mulloch Coire an Iubhair
11/03/2014	149	Creag Pitridh
12/03/2014	150	Mullach Clach a'Bhlair

30/03/2014	151	Seana Bhraigh
31/03/2014	152	Am Faochagach
11/05/2014	153	Sgurr Mhic Choinnich
11/05/2014	154	Sgurr Alasdair
12/05/2014	155	Sgurr Dubh Mor
13/05/2014	156	Sgurr a'Ghreadaidh
13/05/2014	157	Sgurr a'Mhadaidh
15/05/2014	158	Saileag
15/05/2014	159	Sgurr a'Bhealaich Dheirg
15/05/2014	160	Aonach Meadhoin
16/05/2014	161	A'Chralaig
22/05/2014	162	Carn Ghluasaid
22/05/2014	163	Sgurr nan Conbhairean
22/05/2014	164	Sail Chaorainn
23/05/2014	165	Mullach Fraoch-choire
15/06/2014	166	Maoile Lunndaidh
16/06/2014	167	Sgurr na Ruaidhe
16/06/2014	168	Carn nan Gobhar
16/06/2014	169	Sgurr a Choire Ghlais
16/06/2014	170	Sgurr Fuar-thuill
17/06/2014	171	Meall Gorm
19/06/2014	172	Lurg Mhor
19/06/2014	173	Bidean a'Choire Sheasgaich
12/07/2014	174	a'Mharconaich
13/07/2014	175	Braeriach
13/07/2014	176	Sgor an Lochain Uaine
13/07/2014	177	Cairn Toul
13/07/2014	178	The Devil's Point
14/07/2014	179	Beinn Mheadhoin
30/08/2014	180	The Cairnwell
30/08/2014	181	Carn a'Gheoidh
30/08/2014	182	Carn Aosda

31/08/2014	183	Glas Tulaichean
31/08/2014	184	Carn an Righ
01/09/2014	185	Mount Keen
02/09/2014	186	Lochnagar
02/09/2014	187	Carn a'Choire Bhoidheach
02/09/2014	188	Carn an t-Sagairt Mor
02/09/2014	189	Cairn Bannoch
02/09/2014	190	Broad Cairn
04/09/2014	191	Beinn Iutharn Mhor
04/09/2014	192	Carn Bhac
05/09/2014	193	Tolmount
05/09/2014	194	Tom Buidhe
04/10/2014	195	Meall Ghaordaidh
05/10/2014	196	Creag Mhor
05/10/2014	197	Beinn Heasgarnich
06/10/2014	198	Ben Challum
07/10/2014	199	Ben Cruachan
07/10/2014	200	Stob Diamh
08/10/2014	201	Ben More (Mull)
10/10/2014	202	Beinn a'Chleibh
10/10/2014	203	Ben Lui
10/10/2014	204	Ben Oss
10/10/2014	205	Beinn Dubhchraig
11/10/2014	206	Beinn a'Chochuill
11/10/2014	207	Beinn Eunaich
14/10/2014	N/A	Beinn a'Chlaidheimh(demoted)
14/10/2014	208	Sgurr Ban
14/10/2014	209	Mullach Coire Mhic Fhearchair
14/10/2014	210	Beinn Tarsuinn
16/10/2014	211	Beinn a'Chaorainn
16/10/2014	212	Beinn Teallach
17/10/2014	213	Stob Coire Sgriodain

17/10/2014	214	Chno Dearg
25/02/2015	215	Beinn Dorain
26/02/2015	216	Beinn an Dothaidh
19/04/2015	217	Aonach Beag
19/04/2015	218	Beinn Eibhinn
20/04/2015	219	Stob Ban Grey Corries
21/04/2015	220	Beinn na Lap
21/04/2015	221	Sgor Gaibhre
21/04/2015	222	Carn Dearg
23/04/2015	223	Monadh Mor
23/04/2015	224	Beinn Bhrotain
24/04/2015	225	Stob Coire Easain
24/04/2015	226	Stob a'Choire Mheadhoin
10/05/2015	227	Carn a'Mhaim
10/05/2015	228	Derry Cairngorm
12/05/2015	229	Beinn Bhreac
12/05/2015	230	Beinn a'Chaorainn
13/05/2015	231	Beinn a'Bhuird
13/05/2015	232	Ben Avon
15/05/2015	233	Carn an Fhidhleir
15/05/2015	234	An Sgarsoch
17/05/2015	235	Toll Creagach
17/05/2015	236	Tom a'Choinich
18/05/2015	237	Carn Eige
18/05/2015	238	Beinn Fhionnlaidh
18/05/2015	239	Mam Sodhail
20/05/2015	240	Sgurr nan Ceathreamhnan
20/05/2015	241	Mullach na Dheiragain
20/05/2015	242	An Socach
22/05/2015	243	Gleouraich
22/05/2015	244	Spidean Mialach
07/06/2015	245	Sgor na h-Ulaidh

08/06/2015	246	Beinn Mhanach
08/06/2015	247	Beinn Achaladair
08/06/2015	248	Beinn a'Chreachain
09/06/2015	249	Stob a'Choire Odhair
09/06/2015	250	Stob Ghabhar
13/06/2015	251	Carn Dearg
13/06/2015	252	Geal-charn
13/06/2015	253	Ben Alder
13/06/2015	254	Beinn Bheoil
12/07/2015	255	Sron a'Choire Ghairbh
12/07/2015	256	Meall Na Teanga
13/07/2015	257	Sgurr a'Mhaoraich
14/07/2015	258	Sgurr na Ciche
14/07/2015	259	Garbh Chioch Mhor
14/07/2015	260	Sgurr nan Coireachan
14/07/2015	261	Sgurr Mor
16/07/2015	262	Gairich
20/09/2015	263	Stob Coir' an Albannaich
20/09/2015	264	Meall nan Eun
21/09/2015	265	Creise
21/09/2015	266	Meall a'Bhuiridh
22/09/2015	267	Ben Starav
22/09/2015	268	Beinn nan Aighenan
22/09/2015	269	Glas Bheinn Mhor
24/09/2015	270	Beinn Fhionnlaidh
25/09/2015	271	Beinn Sgulaird
27/09/2015	272	Sgurr nan Coirechan
27/09/2015	273	Sgurr Thuilm
28/09/2015	274	Mullach nan Coirean
28/09/2015	275	Stob Ban Mammores
29/09/2015	276	Stob Choire Claurigh
29/09/2015	277	Stob Coire an Laoigh

29/09/2015	278	Sgurr Choinnich Mor
01/10/2015	279	Sgorr Dhearg
01/10/2015	280	Sgorr Dhonuill
02/10/2015	281	Gulvain
31/12/2015	282	Fionn Bheinn